Stress Fracture:

A Memoir of Psychosis

by Tara Meissner

Published by Tara Meissner
Manitowoc, Wisconsin

Edited by Rhonda Clark
Cover design and author photo by Sharon Rucinski

ISBN 978-0-9904951-0-9
Library of Congress Control Number: 2014910761

For Mike

Author's Note

Every illness needs a story. This story is written to give hope, courage, and strength to those who walk along with me. It is written to add another voice to the conversation of mental illness. It is with great care that I put this story on paper in the spirit that it may spark understanding and acceptance – not least of all for me.

People with mental illness often walk silently, too afraid to appear crazy. However, I am more fearful of secrets; I vowed to live my life out loud. With this prose, I have found a whisper that reveals the tragedy of psychosis in the context of a bipolar illness and the hope that treatment offers. My voice is quiet and capable of telling just one story of a disorder that manifests itself uniquely in each person who is afflicted. I aspire to clearly and accurately reflect on an illness that has crippled my mind and efforts to the point of insanity.

As I recovered, I vaguely remembered nonlinear fragments of events that actually occurred during the psychotic break but remembered clearly the voices and lies that pulled me farther out of my mind into a world of distortions where I was a prophet of Christ. This work provides a real view of the misunderstood entrapment of psychosis. Years ago, this loss of self was considered a "nervous breakdown," which was a tidy summary of the cliché "completely lost her mind." As the cracks of insanity started to fracture my being, my family thought I was awake and somewhat lucid. I, however, was trapped in a timeless place somewhere between alert and abyss. For five days, I was secured as an inpatient. For the better part of a year, I fumbled through recovery to find health and self, spirituality and sanity.

Acknowledgements

This book would not be possible without the loving support and care from my husband, Mike.

Missing from the pages of this narrative are my parents, Bruce and Terry Meissner. In reading the pages, it seems like they didn't play a big role in my recovery. Yet they were always there. They took care of my children while I was in the hospital. They picked up my children routinely to join them fishing, to take them shopping, or just to hang out. They would take one or all three depending on how much I could handle. There were several phone calls and conversations with both my mom and dad that helped me sort through the illness and my life in its context. I think they largely are missing from these pages because they are like most parents holding up the scene in the background; no one notices the poles holding up the tent, they just recognize the tent itself. To have written about the poles would have made for a very dry story.

Catherine Egger is a friend like no other. The value of her friendship and the love that was shared around her kitchen table that year is immeasurable. Other friends and relatives also helped in putting me together: Billie Braeger, Heather Gruett, Melissa Paulow, Carol Stodola, Claire Stodola, Tony Stodola, Molly Stodola, Michelle Pike, Jane Babcock, Julie Wesling, Ted Wesling, Sherry Stanek, and a special group of women known as the D.L.A.T.s — Mary Maurer, Lynda Otten, Patty Welnetz, Alanna Kirt, and again Catherine Egger.

I have no memory of the staff at psychiatric care center where I was initially treated, but recognize their ability and skill in dealing with the crisis period. My recovery was possible due to the wise and kind staff at Lakeshore Psychological Associates. Dr. Carducci, thanks for making me cry, laugh, and believe in wellness. Like you said all along, I did get better. Dr. Burbach, thanks for helping me to believe in myself and to not take myself too seriously. You are two angels in my life. Jill, thanks for treating me with kindness and for the candy jar. I appreciate having been treated like a person rather than a patient.

My writing community made this book possible. Amanda Linsmeier was the biggest champion of the work; she never let me give up. Amanda taught me how to write a book, to believe in myself, and allowed me to consider myself as talented with language as she is. Early readers include: Joe Euclide, Norma Bishop, Roxanne Kahn, the late Robin Butler, Kariann Farrey, Catherine Egger, Billie Braeger, Shelley Kubitz, Crystal Otto, Terrance Kilroy, and Katherine Gahl. Later reviewers include: Laura Docter, Melissa Paulow, Dan Kirk, Mary Maurer, Bev Euclide, Bev Denor. Rhonda Clark provided the final copy edit; any remaining errors are my own.

Most importantly are my sons. You give me reason to live and be well. I love you three. You are each my favorite.

Table of Contents

Table of Contents (continued)

PART ONE: THE FOUNDATION

Up North

I wasn't always 33, and I wasn't always crazy. That's the trick of mental illness. It comes and goes, fooling the mind to believe its symptoms are a fluke, a lapse, or a blip on the map of so-called normal life.

No one had ever told me I had bipolar disorder. Not the doctors I saw for depression, not my parents or other relatives, not past lovers, not friends or co-workers, not Mike or the marriage counselors we saw together, not anyone. This mood disorder called bipolar surfaced in young adulthood – staying just long enough to scare me. Then it submerged from view and recognition. It lay dormant and hid beneath the exterior of a normal woman. It played peek-a-boo, never warning when it would erupt and destroy the footholds of productive life.

I grew up in a family of four as the youngest of a pair of daughters. Our family photos are posed shots with forced grins spreading across our faces at the suggestion of the word "cheese" – or to be funny, sometimes "cheese nuggets." Normal, pedestrian even, the pictures suggest. We all have dark brown hair. Growing up I had stringy hair that looked almost black. My sister's hair was thicker and had more caramel tones in it. Dad had black hair, which was full and wavy. Mom gave her fine, straight hair "some shape" with home perms that polluted our kitchen. Dad and I, agreeing the chemical smell was terrible, avoided the makeshift salon with some yard work excuse. My sister, Billie, liked to help Mom and watched as the correct size rollers were selected. It was her job to separate the papers and hand them to my mom, who would lift them over her shoulder to her friend, who would roll a measured strand of flattened hair around a cylinder.

We lived on the western edge of a rural county nestled north of Milwaukee and south of Green Bay. There, I was surrounded by more cows than people. Although agriculture was all around me, the only time I stepped foot in a barn was at the annual county fair. Our closest neighbor was a dairy-farming family. I sometimes played a game of wits with the neighbor boy, seeing who could hold out a blade of grass on the electric fence and pull it away just quickly enough to avoid a shock. There was a pig farm up the road. The crop farmers' endless corn fields were a playground for my sister and me. We built towns with schools, churches, and homes by breaking the stalks to form paths and hideaways. We lost ourselves in those fields on the endless unstructured weekdays of late summer. Unlike my children today, we didn't have scheduled lessons, neighborhoods to bike in, or daycare. We had each other and we had outside.

Many summer weekends were spent Up North. Following a 90-minute drive on the interstate, we weaved through a preserve of towering pine and hardwood forests interspersed with hundreds of lakes and streams. We took several turns on seemingly identical roads, narrow blacktop without a yellow-painted centerline; these country roads were void of curb or gutter and rounded into the sandy edge of the Nicolet Forest. Dad drove relying on muscle memory and instinct, traveling the maze of snaking roads taking us deeper into the woods to a place of privacy. Sitting in the front seat next to him, my mother braced herself and clutched the glove box unable to hide her anxiety about the ride but didn't wear a seat belt. No one wore seat belts then – not even us kids. With each turn, she would just slide closer to my dad across the full-length seat and then back into the door, rolling her eyes but with a hint of joy at the slight danger of it all. There weren't steep ditches, just space for the root systems of trees. Each turn teased my older sister and me that we were almost there.

We anxiously anticipated the turn that would reveal our welcome sign: Grandma's tree. The tree was a huge pine that had persevered more than a hundred years, somehow not sacrificed when the construction crew built the road. Its trunk anchored closer to the road than the stand of trees that began several feet aside it. The evergreen's roadside branches were natural and untouched, therefore canopying a full lane of the rural highway below. This forest side had been trimmed mercilessly to make room for the power lines that came many years after the roads. The result was a lopsided tree that served as a landmark on the way to Grandma and Grandpa's place. Grandma told us from little on that this was her tree; no one questioned this or asked how the tree came to be hers. Sometimes she would cry when she saw it, leaving us unsure if it was because she was sad for the deformed tree or happy that she was nearly home. Grandma Elaine, with red hair and a French Canadian heritage, cried several times a day from an overflow of emotions.

"I cry, because I'm happy," she explained to us until we were old enough to understand that she truly could be so happy tears would spill beautifully from her deep brown eyes down her carefully made-up face.

"There's Grandma's tree!" we cried, knowing our two-hour trip was near its end.

At her tree, we turned off the blacktop streets onto dusty roads that led to a dead-end path. At the third turn, we were a hill away from the trailer. Dad honked the horn to announce our arrival. Billie and I would hurdle ourselves over the back of the front seat and lean over him to get in a few of our own honks. Aunts, uncles, cousins, and Grandma and Grandpa would run to the front yard, waving and blowing kisses to greet us upon our arrival.

My family didn't say "Crivitz" or "the cabin" or even "heading north" for the weekend. Wisconsinites simply said "up north," and this was accepted as a destination – a concrete place, not a direction. Years later, I met a girl in college, the daughter of a logger, who lived year round in rural Marinette County near Crivitz. She informed me the locals referred to us weekenders as "shackers."

Admittedly, it wasn't a vacation home. It was a two-bedroom trailer set on two acres — no water frontage, unless you count the small creek that ran through the property. In my early years, there wasn't indoor plumbing. We brought drinking water in rinsed gallon-sized milk jugs. We used the hose, attached to a ground-water pump, to bathe and fill the dogs' water dishes. In the evening, we children stood in a dish pan filled with an inch of water heated in a tea kettle as our mothers cleaned the day's dirt with a wash cloth. The outhouse had two side-by-side seats on a wooden bench. The double-seat design was superfluous as I can't remember anyone ever using the awful, smelly room with a partner. Sometimes, I'd look in the dark hole below the seat next me and imagine some creature was going to crawl from the abyss or that a snake could slither out to scare me or somehow reach my bare bottom. I clutched the sides of that black plastic seat fiercely, afraid my boney body would fall into the sea of mixed poop and pee, where I would suffocate and die. One summer, a new hole was dug and the "shitter" was moved to rest above the fresh pit. The displaced dirt was used to bury the human waste that had filled the previous dump.

Sometimes, we fished the Peshtigo River or some small, inland lake in hopes of catching perch, bluegills, and crappies. I wished we had a fancy ski boat and envied those families we saw on the water pulling skiers and tubers sporting brightly colored life vests. I sat in an aluminum boat wearing a fluorescent orange tube of a vest, which had dirt and fish and worm goo staining the puffed life preserver that was a size too big and scrunched around my ears.

There were cookouts in the evening on the oversized Texan charcoal grill – barbecued chicken or sirloin steak served with sliced potatoes and onions covered with pats of butter and wrapped in foil; brats and burgers grilled and then kept warm in a bath of beer and onions; and the occasional turkey "roasted" for hours with premade potluck sides. We had free range to drink as many glass bottles of Ting soda as we wanted. We ate from paper plates, which were reinforced with reusable wicker holders.

Following dinner, the men started a bonfire while the women put the food away and washed the dishes. They didn't use the build-a-teepee-and-fill-the-opening-with-twigs-and-leaves method I learned at Girl Scout camp. They lit empty beer cases with a Zippo lighter.

We waited for the waste to ash and the small branches to catch and fuel the logs. Then we roasted marshmallows. I burnt mine, preferring the confection completely charred. I held the stick over an open flame and watched the marshmallow swell and blister until its surface was black. I pulled it out abruptly to blow out the flame, often losing the flimsy treat in the pit to bubble and melt on a hot log. Disappointed but determined, I started again with the same process, only removing the stick slower from the flame to bring the torched treat to my face to blow out the flame. My sister patiently roasted her marshmallows well above a glowing ember, spinning her stick smoothly to get an even tan with some darker blisters of brown encasing a gooey perfection. The pair of us presented our marshmallows to Dad to see which kind he liked better. More often, he chose the charred variety, which I took as a confirmation that I was his favorite daughter. Mom reminded us that she "hated" marshmallows, though we still offered her some every time. We used found sticks that my dad sharpened with his pocket knife; there were no manufactured wired forks to use.

Well past our bedtimes, we watched the blaze in the fire pit, six feet in diameter with a double ring of cinder blocks. After the roasting was done, the fire was built to epic heights. And, we could always count on Jeff, who we called Uncle French Fry, to try to jump from one end of the pit to the other. Sometimes he made it and sometimes ... well, let's just say his legs are well scarred.

"Kids, don't try that. Ever!" my mother warned.

"That is right," Dad added. "Do what I say not what I do."

Chuckles erupted from the around the pit, where we sat on lawn chairs and picnic tables with adjacent mismatched TV trays for drinks. Some sat on couches that were lined up for future fires. Over the years, the fire pit became a burial ground for old couches, cracked recliners, retired mattresses, and tires. Every discarded object was up for consideration to haul to the trailer just to see how big of a fire we could make. There seemed to be a competition among the men as to whom could bring the object that would create the highest or most interesting flame — and each cousin cheered on their father for the braggin' rights. Year after year, though, nothing topped the bowling ball. While its blaze wasn't impressive in size, the found object burned for hours and gave off florescent yellow, blue, and green flames. Each layer of the ball created new mixtures of color and flame. I think if you ask any Meissner today, they would remember that summer night when we tossed a bowling ball into the fire.

As it grew dark, the clarity of the unencumbered sky made a beautiful display of stars. Dad would point out the

Big Dipper, Orion, and the planet Venus. Classic rock music was piped from a stereo console in the living room, its speakers balanced in window sills.

From the trees, we heard whippoorwills. Dad whistled "woop der do whoo" and the birds answered his skillful call. I tried to echo the call, but ended up humming the sound, which made the adults laugh. The adults sat around that fire getting louder and louder well after the cousins were piled in a spare bedroom with bunks, or in tents and campers. Mom went into the trailer to mix another rum and coke for herself as well as a brandy and water for Grandma Elaine; I heard the ice cubes, cracked from an aluminum tray, clink the glasses. My dad, his brothers and sisters, and accompanying in-laws grabbed cans of beer from one of the two refrigerators stored in a garden shed. These were plugged into a string of extension cords fed from the three-pronged outlet on the utility pole at the roadside.

The men also went Up North in the fall to hunt deer, but no one generally went there during the winter months; Grandma and Grandpa were snow birds who spent winter months in Florida. But one year, following a big storm, our family went with my aunt's family to check on some damage caused by the storm.

In December of my fifth-grade year, a cousin and I bundled into snow pants, winter coats, and boots. We had a series of foot races down a hill and up the next to the end of the road by my grandparents' trailer. The hills were steep and separated by a narrow valley – perfect for learning about gravity and momentum while riding bicycles in the summer.

With the bikes tucked in a locked shed, we raced on foot down and up the ice-covered dirt hills. I was leading by a couple of strides. My cousin was gaining on me when I was halfway up the incline. My Spaniel-mix, Sparky, suddenly barreled from the woods and crossed my path in perfect time to trip up my step. I landed hard with my left hand outstretched on the cold, frozen ground. My cousin darted past me, certain of his victory. Winded at the top of the hill, he turned and saw me curled on the ground. When I noticed him looking at me, I stood up, shrugged, and shouted "Rematch!"

My wrist throbbed, but we raced several more times before being called inside to get ready to leave. I didn't tell my parents about the fall or the hurt wrist because the pain was manageable. It was easy enough to hide … until it wasn't.

That night back at home, the pain in my wrist became too much to ignore. I screamed for my mother from my bed, increasing my volume with every "Mom" I cried.

Groggily, she came to my side. I told her to turn on the bedroom light and held up my arm.

"What?" she said.

"My wrist hurts," I told her.

Then she realized it was swollen.

"What did you do?" she asked.

"I fell," I said. "It really hurts."

"When did you fall?"

"At Grandma's. I was racing," I said. "I tripped over Sparky."

"Why didn't you say something earlier? Can you move it?"

I tried to move it but couldn't. Mom shook her head, rolled her eyes, and left the room. She came back with a plastic bag filled with ice cubes and a kitchen towel.

"Put this on it," she said. "If it is still swollen in the morning, I'll take you to the doctor."

The next day, an X-ray confirmed a hair-line fracture. That injury was clear and simple — easy to diagnose and treat and heal.

Years later, I would suffer a stress fracture, though not in the orthopedic sense. The stress that pressured a scission wasn't physical. The matter that forced a break was intangible. My mind, adapting in its own large, grey blob of substance, separated ever so slightly over time until it formed a chasm between sanity and insanity.

School Days

My mother liked to tell the story about the time she had mono when I was 3 years old. With her debilitated with mono, my 6-year-old sister and I were asked to become more independent. Mom apparently asked us to help by doing the dishes: Billie washed and I dried and put away. It seemed I felt it was an incredible injustice to never get a turn to wash.

As the story went, I told my mother — and this part was an alleged direct quote from my preschool mouth — "Life isn't going to be easy for me."

This story was told over and over again throughout my childhood, although I had no memory of it. And it was funny to everyone who heard it. Apparently, I was determined to prove it true. I fulfilled the prophetic words from my young mouth, and forged ahead with a life that wasn't easy and carried a strong conviction that life was not fair.

Whether it was the "prophecy" I'd made, or whether it was purely coincidence, I failed to do well in school both socially and academically. Later in life, this would display in an unstable job history where I was unable to win awards or keep friends.

In kindergarten, I felt I was slighted by getting the wrong teacher. Mrs. Cooper was the good teacher. I got the other one; I can't remember her name. My teacher was older, more no-nonsense, and rumored to be mean. She had a wrinkled face and wore frumpy clothes. Mrs. Cooper was young, energetic, and dressed in colorful jumpers. Our side of the partitioned room had the bathrooms and the door that led to the playground. From there we could see Mrs. Cooper's class line up in the hallway to go to their recess; everyone was well behaved. I was not.

One day I hit and kicked a classmate because she budged when we were lining up for music class. Our teacher pulled us both from line and made us sit on the ledge beneath the coat rack. This was not a seating area, but rather a designated spot for holding snow boots. While the rest of our classmates learned to keep a steady beat, we sat silently separated by a few feet of space with our hands to ourselves.

By first grade, I was enrolled in special education classes. In 1981, they called it Chapter One. This was designed to improve my reading. A handful of the "slow" kids went to the only room in the school with computers, the kind with green letters and a blinking green box for a cursor on a black screen.

By third grade, I was pulled from classes to meet with a guidance counselor. These meetings were my first structured intervention to my "behavior" problems. Sometimes we met one-on-one to talk; other times we would gather with my peers who also were labeled troublemakers. I didn't receive any sort of psychological diagnosis — it was the early 1980s. As it was, I was just a pest who needed to learn self-control and good decision making skills. If my behaviors then were symptoms of mental illness, they weren't named or recognized. If bipolar existed then, it was disguised as poor attitude, short temper, moodiness, impatience, and other personality flaws.

My report cards were filled with negative remarks both in conduct and in coursework. When I learned cursive writing, I received my first failing grade for penmanship. My parents were told I rushed through my work, I was sloppy, and didn't care. I didn't think that was true, but the school staff had grown tired of my excuses. I thought I was trying but couldn't master the precision required to gently form the bellies of the letters B, P, or lower case g. The fluid connection of the letters from one to the other was another area of struggle; I mixed printing with the cursive and my words had breaks. On later report cards, I was identified as an excessive talker who disrespected authority; I was easily distracted, messy, and didn't use class time well; worst of all, they said, I wasn't living up to my potential. Once report cards went computerized, these canned phrases populated the comment squares in random order next to each subject, placed there by teachers who already had me pegged.

The silly blacken-the-oval-corresponding-to-the-correct-answer standardized tests would contradict my performance in the classroom. These marks would place me above the 90th percentile of my peers. This conundrum was a source of frustration for me, for my teachers, and for my parents. I was disciplined regularly, unlike my sister who mastered everything placed in front of her and seemed to take pride in her report card comments: "commendable effort," "pleasure to have in class," and "strong student."

My fourth-grade teacher didn't help when she wouldn't call on me when I kept raising my hand. I did it while she was talking.

"Tara, put your hand down," Mrs. Z said.

I did, wiggled in my seat and then shot my hand back up.

"Tara, put your hand down," Mrs. Z said.

This continued for several minutes until finally I gave up and peed in my pants. As a fourth-grader's bladder can hold quite a bit, this created a puddle and generated some laughter before attracting Mrs. Z's attention. On her order to go to the office, I cleaned up and changed into some school clothes donated for these types of purposes. (Generally these clothes were intended for smaller kids, but I was small for my age and squeezed into a pair of someone else's underwear and burgundy corduroys.)

This was my most embarrassing, cringe-worthy moment for years to come. Looking back, I find it funny now. At the time, I didn't want to return to the classroom. I was one of two of Mrs. Z's students who peed in their pants that year. The other boy was heavy for his age and had to spend the rest of the day wearing snow pants. In that regard, I was grateful for my size and for the school's donated clothing.

To my extreme annoyance, Mrs. Z also called me by Billie's name repeatedly. (Today, I have children who look alike and even I mix up their names, so I can see how this could happen.) Then, I thought she just did it to piss me off. It seemed everyone was always trying to piss me off. I practiced passive aggressive disobedience when she called on me. If she would use my sister's name, I'd ignore her. She would get frustrated and say Billie again. I would then turn and look behind me, pretending to look for my sister. This charade could continue for minutes, until she realized her innocent blunder and that I was punishing her.

One day, she really slipped and said, "Why can't you just be more like your sister?"

Certainly she wasn't the first or the last to make that comparison, but she was definitely the only one to say it out loud. This comment was more damaging to my ego than pants wetting, but my peers didn't see it as obviously tease-worthy, so it didn't follow me socially like wetting myself did. I just carried a belief that I was less than good enough and unworthy of love and respect.

Likewise, I couldn't respect the system. I couldn't work in the confines of an institution. Neat rows and prescribed instructions didn't facilitate learning for me. And, I didn't belong among my peers who were largely content and happy to perform for the adults in this box-like setting. I felt uncomfortable every time I walked through the fluorescent-lit halls. My childhood nicknames were "Tara the Terrible" and "Tara the Bear."

I found my identity in becoming the troublemaker my authorities said I was. In sixth grade, I didn't go out for recess often. By then, I was considered old enough to know better and was punished with detentions, which I served regularly. I was not allowed to eat in the gymnasium-turned-cafeteria for lunch. I'd carry my lunch room tray – plastic, hard, and partitioned – to Mrs. B's classroom, and sit at my desk. No talking was the rule. In the upper right hand corner of the blackboard was my name, two check marks behind it. I didn't have to tell my mother about this rule breaking; that required four check marks for a notice home. Above and below my name were other names – these were the names of my friends. One would supply me with my first cigarette, though I lied and told her I already smoked. In a way, I was proud of my non-conforming behaviors. With them, I found an identity and others who were like me. I could feel comfortable with these friends – they didn't pick on me, didn't get mad when I talked too much, and didn't put expectations on me.

While the good kids may have played four-square or paged through BOP magazines during lunch recess, I sat and ate my bulk-prepared food in a desk that was in a neat row. I picked chocolate milk over white from the plastic, orange crates and would look over the pictures of missing children stamped on the sides of the cartons, wondering what would happen if I went missing. I often daydreamed of a better life waiting for me someplace other than where I was. The library had a poster that said, "Bloom where you are planted," but I didn't agree. I wanted to be anywhere else. I wanted to run away.

Chasing Chickens

Dad was a union laborer, and in the 1980s there were times he would be laid off and the unemployment checks didn't seem to go far enough to support our family. He remained loyal to an iron foundry and would stand by steady for the call back notice when castings were again in demand. Each year he worked, he gathered another rung on the seniority ladder, climbing for another week of paid vacation and the promised pension contributions. He learned this work ethic from his father, who spent his adulthood after WWII with a manufacturing company. A proud man who provided well for his family of 10 with his wife Elaine at his side, Grandpa Ken died a few short years into retirement at the age of 69.

My mother suffered from rheumatoid arthritis, and the cost of her medical treatment complicated our financial picture. After the deterioration of her joints made physical labor no longer possible, she decided to put her vocational efforts into mothering us girls. She had been a cook at a family restaurant, and became a homemaker. She was the leader of my Girl Scout troop. She liked to bake and prepared home-cooked meals every evening. Mom had a room of her own, a sewing room where she sewed us clothes – sometimes matching from the same fabric. Other times, she made detailed clothes for our Barbie dolls from the scraps.

Mom returned to school and graduated magna cum laude the year I graduated from high school without honors. She went on to chair the math and computer science departments at an area high school. Years prior, poverty crippled our family, yet it never devastated us. I grew up respecting hard work and believing the American dream was tangible. The trials we experienced were just that, and as the saying goes, they made us stronger.

My first opportunity for work surfaced in 7th grade when I heard a blurb in the morning announcements at school. The job was at a nearby egg farm and paid $7.50 for two hours of work. I eagerly signed my name on a loose leaf page of paper next to the three upcoming dates, unsure what the job itself would entail. A bus full of junior high and high school workers were to be shuttled to and from the egg farm located roughly two miles south of school.

The problem with this arrangement was my mother needed to pick me up at the school around 5:30 p.m. Mom hesitated; she never liked to drive us anywhere. Plus, she worried, asking me again and again if I would get hurt. But I didn't have the answer and was too focused on making money to buy the extras my parents couldn't afford, like cool clothes and by then, the occasional cigarette. Without much ammunition to combat my stubbornness, she finally relented.

When the scheduled day came, I boarded the bus with mostly guys. None of the teachers' children were in the bunch, I noted (which made sense, since I perceived the teachers' children to be rich). My other idea of what was rich was my friends who had name-brand cereal in colorful boxes with prizes inside. My mom stocked our cupboard with generic frosted flakes and crispy rice, which came in large white boxes with heavy black lettering within a stamped rectangle. Not having name-brand food, or even enough food sometimes, made me feel less worthy than those families with stable incomes. However, Mom didn't skimp on everything. She always purchased Jif peanut butter and Kraft Macaroni and Cheese rather than their generic alternatives, but would stretch our milk by adding a half gallon of mixed powdered milk. I got hair cuts from a friend of my mom's in the kitchen, and Mom trimmed my bangs unevenly between those haircuts. I wore hand-me downs from my sister; my shoes, however, were always new, purchased a size too big to make them last.

As I started my teen years, I decided I needed to make an income. My sister began babysitting at this age, but I didn't get asked very much. The bus was full of other kids in a similar situation. When we came upon the farm located on a back road, it was my first time seeing the chicken farm. I looked out the school bus windows in awe of the barn, yard, and large white house. There were a handful of men wearing work clothes standing around outside the bus. As I waited for the rows of seats in front of me to empty, a familiar swirl of uneasiness settled in my stomach. Then, I stood in a makeshift half circle with the "crew" until the last child exited the bus to join us on the gravel driveway.

"A shipment of chickens will be arriving by truck any minute," the farm owner told us. "Your job is to get them from the truck to the barn."

He didn't tell us about the stench. He didn't give us a training video. I was unprepared for the actual process of transporting a load of chickens. When the truck came, and the driver opened the back and placed a ramp down, I saw wire cages were stacked on top of one another. Here I was wearing my school clothes; I was not even wearing work boots. Through trial and error and watching the older boys work, I soon learned the best way to carry a chicken was by its legs.

The chickens, meanwhile, flapped their wings frantically in the chaotic setting. We hadn't been told chickens would look for an opportunity to escape and run around the barnyard, though this clearly made sense. I felt bad for those chickens who wanted freedom, whose fate was to be let out of one cage just to be put in another.

As I carried the chickens by their feet, their heads swung back and forth dangerously close to the ground. I was not tall, so I had to bend my elbows and lift the chickens up to protect their heads from being dragged on the ground or banged on the steps to the second story of the barn. There were rows of wire homes, which opened at the top. I ran back and forth, up and down, and through the maze of rows of cages from truck to barn repeatedly. The process took all of the two hours of steady, mindless, strenuous to and fro. By the end, I was sweating and covered with chicken feathers and droppings. My petite arms ached. My legs burned.

Suddenly the pittance of a wage didn't seem such a prize for all the catching, lugging, and stair climbing I endured in an attempt to create order in a land of chaos. My young frame was exhausted. I didn't honor the future dates on the egg farm work calendar, deciding to leave it for those poor souls who were stronger and hungrier than me.

Boundaries

My freshman and sophomore years of high school were fairly uneventful. While my peers had boyfriends and parties to go to, I didn't. I studied and was finally making good on the potential my earlier teachers said I had. But I was bored. I wanted some excitement in my life. As it happened, I turned to trouble again pretty much by accident.

The summer before my junior year, a pizza place for teens opened across the street from my high school. The building had been a candy store in the past, but was vacant for some time. There was always this argument that teens needed something to do or a place to be to keep them out of trouble. The only problem was these types of places always attracted the kids who didn't have a place to go or something to do.

When the business opened, I had my first regular job. My responsibilities included serving pizza and ice cream to my peers and I had to sweep and mop before locking up. These were the basics of the job; I naively thought those were the only duties of the job. The cash from the day's sales were stored in a Tupperware container in the freezer, which locked. We didn't accept credit cards; the handy swipers of today were not the norm at small businesses in the early 1990s.

My friends from 6th grade, who I hadn't hung out with for a while, visited me while I worked. I always charged them full price for food, but usually they didn't have any money, so they would just hang out. All in all, I felt pretty good about the job. I made enough weekly to supply what became my regular habits of smoking and drinking.

When some of the kids from rougher crowds started to patronize the store, I became a little uncomfortable. Wanting to appear "cool," I didn't say anything. I would eventually get to know this other group of kids and consider them friends. I became a drinker pretty much the same way I became a smoker: I lied saying I already was one. That summer, we were always looking for "cool" people to hang out with. I didn't know Miranda well, but her parents worked during the day so her house was unsupervised. One afternoon, I drove my friend Tammy there to "hang out." A couple of other kids were at Miranda's as well. I wanted to be accepted. So when they asked me if I drank, I lied and said yes. They didn't believe me. I complicated the story by telling them my older sister got me drunk, which hadn't happened. Still unconvinced, they wanted proof.

"What do you drink?" Tammy asked.

"Brandy," I thought out loud on my feet probably because Grandma Elaine was a faithful drinker of brandy and water and it was the first mixed drink to come to mind.

The kids laughed at me.

"I have some brandy in the cupboard," Miranda said. "How about I mix you a brandy and coke?"

"Sure," I said, unsure of what would happen, but wanting to prove I was a drinker.

They took out a "Moose" cup from Hardee's. The Moose cup was a cheap plastic, oversized cup that held a terrific amount of soda. Miranda took to mixing me a drink.

I had two.

Naturally, I passed out. The story got retold throughout the next two years of high school. As the story went, my friends loaded me in the back of Miranda's mom's old mini van and drove me around, stopping at various people's houses to show off the fact that I couldn't hold my liquor. I sort of woke up when we got back to Miranda's. My friends half carried me inside and put me on the kitchen floor. I got a sneezing attack; I sneezed so hard my head would lift from the linoleum floor and slam back down hard. Snot flew everywhere. I knew this, because the story spread throughout the entire school and everyone who signed my yearbook the next two years commented on the hilarity of it all.

My mother was a responsible person who always asked for the phone number of our friends' houses before I could go there. When the wall phone rang, Miranda answered it and heard my mother on the other end. Suddenly a round of hushes and shushes and giggles in the background quieted the noise.

"Tara's in the barn. She can't come to the phone right now," Miranda said.

"Tara wants to go to a movie with us. Can she come? "

"Umm, I'm not sure what movie."

"Tara's fine."

Someone placed the phone by my ear.

"Ask your mom if you can go to the movies with us tonight," someone said.

"Movie. Can. I," I said.

"Are you okay?" my mother said.

"Yeah," I laughed. "I'm fine."

"Well you don't sound all right. I'm coming to get you. Where does Miranda live?"

"I'm not sure," I said. "Where do you live, Miranda?"

Not wanting to get into trouble, they took the phone and tried to dissuade my mom from coming to get me. It was no use; they eventually rattled off the address and doled out directions.

"Tara, your mom is on the way. You have to pull it together."

I laughed. My friends were scheming ways to hide my drunkenness; they fed me bread dipped in bulk tank milk and told me it would make me puke. It was no use. I couldn't move from my flat-on-my-back position on the kitchen floor, where they had dropped me earlier.

When Mom arrived, she pushed through my friends to form a path to me and saw me.

"My God, what happened to you? What did you take?"

"Brandy," I said, pretty proud of my exploration.

"This can't be just brandy. What else did you take?"

"Coke," I said.

"My God, you took cocaine?!" my mother said, ever the extremist.

My friends might have laughed, but they reassured her and said I just got like this and came over with the brandy myself. They were in save-my-own-ass mode.

"No, soda," I laughed again.

With the help of my friends, I was loaded into the passenger seat of my mom's car. One friend volunteered to drive my car home, and Miranda agreed to follow us there with her mom's van to bring everyone back to her house. So the caravan began.

About a half-mile down the gravel road, I felt bubbles in my stomach. I couldn't talk. I reached for the door handle, opened it and rolled out of the car, tumbling from the gravel to the ditch with long grass, where I puked and puked and puked. Somehow I didn't kill myself.

When we got home, my mother considered taking me to the hospital. I didn't know if it was my pleas to not go or if it was her own embarrassment of her daughter, but she didn't take me. I vomited some more in the bathroom, was given a large glass of water and put to bed. The bed spun or maybe it was the room. I remembered Grandma Elaine once saying she sometimes swung a leg over to the floor to stop bed spins. At that moment, I knew what she was talking about, and it worked.

I was grounded for a few weeks, but my friends had successfully initiated me to the drinkers' crowd. From that point forward and through the rest of my high school career, they were right there to take me out to beer parties in the woods of someone's house, in the middle of a country road, places that were supposedly haunted, or at the gravel pits that were abandoned in the night. My parents always were told I was watching movies with my friends, yet I'm sure they knew and looked the other way when I became mixed with the drinking crowd.

Regarding the job at the pizza place — well one day, I was fired, abruptly, with no explanation. Turns out, the owner was coming up short on the money rang through the register, and he assumed I was taking it. He was wrong; I hadn't taken a dime. But I also had no idea how to make it right, or who would have taken the money.

Really, any number of people who I called friends that summer could have stolen the money. I guess the job also involved a little gate keeping – boundaries, if you will. Anyway, I wasn't attracting the right kind of customers to the establishment. Nor was I repelling the wrong ones to the store or really to me.

Insane Asylum

My first glimpse of psychiatric care was a chance ride with a fellow student to an abandoned insane asylum in my sophomore year of college. George, who had three first names but went by his middle name, and I were smoking cigarettes riding around in his worn down Pontiac, which had a cracked windshield.

"Do you want to see something cool?" he asked, as we drove aimlessly through the city streets.

"Sure," I said.

As we drove outside the Oshkosh city limits, I began to feel the familiar friend of queasiness sputter in my stomach, which signaled the need for caution. This wasn't the first anxiety I felt, but I didn't know enough to classify it as such.

"Where are we going?" I asked with trepidation.

I realized I knew this man, whom I had a crush on, solely from my interactions with others who I knew only from the first two months of classes. George was cool with long straggly hair and baggy clothes. He hung out with other students from the third floor of Fletcher Hall.

My freshman year of college, I lived on an all girls floor of a quiet dorm. I requested the transfer to Fletcher Hall because it had a reputation for being a "party" dorm. I blamed my external surroundings for my unhappiness with the college scene. I thought a change of scenery would offer a chance to enjoy the college experience. This was part of my Achilles' heel: "I will be happy when ..." I kept changing my settings, chasing that place where I could conform comfortably.

"You will see," he said to me as he confidently navigated some country roads.

I relaxed and we turned our attention to the Pink Floyd disc playing from his car stereo as we made several turns deeper in the country.

We came upon an abandoned institution with a locked gate at the asphalt path that circled to the front of the building. This driveway was littered with downed branches, and cracks of growth began to emerge from the once pristine entrance.

"What is this place?"

"This is where they locked away the crazies."

Long abandoned, the building was a treatment center for the mentally ill who were committed voluntarily and for those on the county's vulnerable list who had no place else to go. Paranoid panic overtook me.

"Get me out of here!" I said. "Why would you take me here?"

"Whoa, calm down. We can leave. I just think it's cool in a creepy kind of way," George said.

"It's just creeping me out. Were you going to leave me here?"

"What? No, of course not. I just thought you'd like to see it. It was just something to see," he said. "Can you believe they locked people far away from civilization?"

"I thought you said we are leaving," I said, with panic in my voice.

My breathing was heavy with sporadic gasps; I looked over my shoulder.

"We shouldn't be here," I said through quiet lips.

"I'm waiting for this car and then I'll turn around," George said.

"What car? Is there a car? Is it a cop? Are we supposed to be here? Are we going to get arrested?" I rushed out what I know now were illogical questions.

"Calm down, there is no reason to freak out," George said.

He turned the car and made his way back to the university. He parked in the campus lot blocks from the dormitories. He walked me to the door of the 10-story brick structure, where my 15 x 15 room awaited. He didn't ask to come up; I didn't invite him in. I rushed up the stairs, afraid of the elevator, to my fourth-floor room, and made my way down the hall to the last room on the right.

I fumbled for keys and entered the mess, which was my room. I sat on my bed and bowed my head into my hands, relieved he didn't leave me at the insane asylum and embarrassed that I ruined our evening with a paranoid panic attack. Certain I wouldn't hear from the cool and calm George again, I cursed myself for my stupidity. Why did I let such things frighten me?

Fortunately I had a single room. Unfortunately, this had resulted from the time I was arrested for domestic violence for slapping my Greek-entrenched slut roommate Tricia. She was rushing Phi Blah Blah Blah. She fit the sorority sister stereotype neatly and enjoyed hooking up with guys from the frat houses. One night, someone wrote "Fat Whore lives here" on the dry erase board hanging outside our door. Immediately, she realized it was directed at her.

"Do you think I am fat?" she had asked then.

"No, I think you're a whore," I had said in all seriousness.

To say we didn't get along was an understatement. I was aimless and lacked ambition, and had dreadlocks, which I died purple. She dressed trendy, wore too much makeup, and loved to socialize. One Tuesday, before an 11:30 biology class, a couple of my friends were hanging in our dorm room.

My five-disc changer shuffled songs from the Grateful Dead, Tom Petty, Cat Stevens, Simon and Garfunkel, and Jimmy Buffet.

Tricia was getting pissed. She was getting ready for a comp class and couldn't find the paper I had written for her the night before. It was right on her desk. I wrote papers for her, because I wanted her to like me. I wanted to feel useful. I wanted approval.

"I can't find a thing in this place. You and your friends NEED to stop hanging out in here," she shouted.

"Whoa, take it easy," I said.

Without warning, she grabbed my fan from the window and smashed it into the Sony stereo I had bought with excess student loan money. The event was like in slow motion, as I tried to stop her. It was no use; her actions were too quick to bring to a halt. The music sputtered and stopped. Pleased with herself, she slapped her hands on her thighs.

"You bitch," I said, and lunged toward her, possessed with revenge.

Cursed with an eruption of uncontrollable rage, I slapped her open palm across her blush-stained cheek. Immediately, the remorse hit.

"Whoa, sorry, man. I don't know where that came from."

She dismissed me, picked up her paper, stuffed it in her designer knapsack and left the room, opening the door and causing our smoke to escape into the hallway. I ushered my friends out, pulled on a pair of shoes, and left for Bio 101. As I sat in class, I replayed the event while I doodled in a notebook.

Really, she had it coming, but the rage that overtook me had scared me. After class I aimlessly walked on campus, picking up a disposable cup of coffee from the campus union store and then walking to the neighborhood smoke shop, where I picked up a hard pack of Camel lights.

I returned to an empty room, and tried to get my stereo to work. It did. I sat on the couch mulling over a sincere and sober apology waiting for Tricia to return. I knew her class schedule and was expecting her any time. She didn't come. Instead, I heard a rap on the door.

"Come in," I called from my seat on the couch.

"We need you to open the door," a male voice replied.

Through the peep hole, I recognized the people outside as campus police. I opened the door slowly.

"Are you Tara Meissner?"

"Yes."

"We need to see some identification."

I walked to my dresser and pulled my Student ID card, which was stamped with my social security number. They held it on a clipboard.

"We're here to ask you a few questions," one of the pseudo cops said. "Can you tell me what happened today?"

The entire story gushed from my mouth. I was shocked by what came next.

"We're going to have to take you downtown," the other said.

"Nooo, you can't. I said I was sorry. It was just a mistake. We will work it out," I pled.

"She filed a report. Because you two live together, we have to treat this as a domestic violence offense and one of you has to be arrested. There will be a 72-hour restraining order. You admitted to being the aggressor."

I was hauled down in a squad car after parading past students who shared my dormitory. I was ducked into the backseat of the squad with handcuffs restraining my arms behind my back. I was booked: the whole deal, with mug shots and finger prints. Then, I was locked in a barred box with a hard bed on the cinder block wall and an exposed toilet in the opposite corner. My one phone call was to my mother who came to post the bail. She rescued me. My record would ultimately document a disorderly conduct and came with a fine, which my parents paid. Another result: I was barred from Fletcher Hall dormitory and deemed unable to have a roommate; I was assigned a single room in a dorm across campus.

In my single room, I locked my door and closed the shades. Looking in my fridge revealed empty shelves. I wanted some water, but was afraid to go out to the common bubbler down the hallway, still thinking of the abandoned mental institution. I put on a sweat suit and crawled into bed, covers pulled over my head.

**

College in general was a bust, a failed opportunity. I went to college, because it promised a freedom pass from physical labor. I attended UW-Oshkosh, because it was the only college I applied to on a whim and no one was more surprised than me when I was accepted. I entered college with an undeclared major. I later changed my major to nursing, and then to art when chemistry kicked my ass leaving me with a CD for the course, not high enough to get admission to the school of nursing. I retook chemistry in hopes of improving my grade, but the second time through I sunk to a D. Damn academia didn't fit right. Fucking achievement was beyond my capacity.

George and I met in the same social rings as before, but a romance never bloomed. We never mentioned the country road drive to each other again and I hoped he didn't mention it to others either. Because of the "domestic violence" incident, I wasn't allowed to go back to Fletcher Hall where he lived.

I rarely went to class, and I told my family and hometown friends I was majoring in underwater basket weaving. I spent the rest of my sophomore year at a coffee shop, where I could smoke my Camels indoors and sit for hours. Others studied at the coffee house while I filled my class notebooks with more doodles.

I wasn't failing all my classes; with little effort I was able to garner some Cs. I did try in my creative writing class and received an AB, the highest mark of my two-year college career. I really believed I was trying, but I also believed I was cursed. Dad would say, "Of course it's hard, but you can do it. You can do anything you set your mind to." Mom echoed his endorsement. Only I couldn't. I couldn't set my mind to something. I couldn't achieve. I never won an award my entire life. I never received an honor.

I dropped out of college. I was too proud to admit I essentially failed; I left, in part, because I felt out of my skin in the confining dorm spaces. I didn't want to be trapped in a room and a place where I didn't belong. When I returned home, I explained that I left due to finances and said I wanted to join the Army to get the GI education benefits.

Pill-induced sleep

I was ejected from the MEPS building. The MEPS building is where we gathered before being shipped to basic training. The acronym stands for Military Entrance Processing Station. This was where I was to have my one last physical and drug test before moving on to Fort Leonard Wood in Missouri. After the six weeks of training, I was going to get AIT (Advanced Individual Training) in medical records at a Texas base. I was enlisted as an E2 rather than an E1 because of my college experience. I hoped this would be my ticket out of Wisconsin and back into college with funding from the GI bill.

At the MEPS, the women were segregated from the men. We sat in lines and waiting-room chairs for long periods of time. The night before, I spent a sleepless night in the Howard Johnson. I skipped the provided continental breakfast so I could make weight. I was supposed to weigh less than 145 pounds at my height of 5'7". There were the routine checks; we had to do the "duck walk" dressed in bras and underwear to make sure we didn't have flat feet. Following this exercise, I sat on a hard bench sans external clothing, which would have provided a stitch of modesty. When my name was called: "MEISSNER," I walked across the linoleum-covered holding pen and was placed on an examining table; no gown was provided. I was exposed in front of a cherub, elderly man and overweight smirk-faced, female nurse. The man, who seemed a bit more gleeful than professional, conducted a breast exam. He was presumably checking for the long shot of lumps in my 20-year-old body. The nurse then stepped up to watch him perform a pelvic exam.

Prior to this invasion against my body, I had had my vision and hearing checked fully clothed. The routine blood pressure and temperature tests were uneventful. We were escorted through lines marked with ribbons marking the winding paths like those used in a theme park for popular rides. We weaved back and forth, before having been put in the holding pen. One of the checks in the holding pen was a weight check performed in our undergarments. The scale measured my weight at 146. I knew this was over the limit. Yet, they didn't kick me out right away – they put me through the rest of the processing checks. I thought I would just have a harder time at basic; I wasn't prepared for the actual events that took place.

After my exam in the room, I was released back to the room with the other girls in their underwear. We waited for the last girl to have her exam. All the girls were dismissed to the locker room and from there we all went to a waiting area for a shuttle to awaiting flights to basic training sites. I was placed in another waiting room chair outside the military officers' rooms. As my name was called, I stood at attention, like we had been trained to do in the morning.

"You didn't make weight," the sergeant said to me.

"I think I'm getting my period; my weight fluctuates; it is only a pound, I can lose it at Basic," justifications gushed out of my mouth.

No matter. He pulled the two-inch file with my photo stapled on its cover and opened it. Grabbing a rubber stamp, he dabbed it in red ink and stamped the word "obese" in capital letters on the cover page of the file. He didn't stop there. This five-inch word was stamped again and again on page after page of my file.

"You are free to go home. We will arrange transportation," the sergeant said.

I rode on a Greyhound bus from downtown Milwaukee to Appleton, approximately 40 miles from my parents' home in Reedsville. The bus ride was full of stops and starts with questionable passengers boarding. I hugged my duffle filled with plain white underclothes and basic toiletries tight, irrationally afraid of theft. I cried and cried. There are no words for the shame that came on that ride back to the life I just thought I had a ticket to leave.

Before I went to processing, my parents had thrown me a going away party where family and friends had wished me well and bought me gifts. Proud that I would be following in his father's footsteps, Dad had given me a cross his dad wore around his neck in WWII. My father himself didn't serve in his generation's conflict in Vietnam, but held the conviction that it would have been a great honor to my family to have me serve in the United States Military.

I called my parents collect from a gas station in Appleton, the closest stop to my rural home. While I waited for them to pick me up, I walked back and forth as I considered an explanation. All I could think was: I failed again, I was a failure. I let them down. I embarrassed my family and myself, because I was fat.

They came and got me. They asked questions, and I cried in return. I couldn't face the truth; I crawled into myself. Exhausted from a sleepless night in the hotel, a grueling eight-hour day processing at the MEPS, a degrading Greyhound shuttle, and the disgraceful ride home in my father's pickup truck, I immediately crashed in my bed.

"I'm beat," I said as an explanation.

My parents indulged me, leaving me to wallow in self pity.

Sometime later, I groggily walked to my parents' kitchen cabinet where the over-the-counter medications were held. I found some sleeping pills and took a handful. I knew it wasn't enough to kill myself, but the idea of death at my own hands was tempting. I had nowhere to go. I was back in my parents' house – the house I was supposed to leave at the magic age of 18. Yet it would become a boomerang safety net for me time and again throughout my young adult life.

There was nothing I could do to stop the shame and pain, so I returned to the bed to wait for the comfort of sleep to again numb all feeling. Why that cupboard was stocked with sleeping pills is an answer I'll never know, but its respite from life was a place I returned to day after day. With a glass of water, I washed away wakefulness that brought back my recent memories of suffering. I could not shake the shame and embarrassment. I was humiliated. I wanted to be like the groundhog and hide until it all went away. I couldn't face my life. I couldn't look at my failures. I couldn't find my face to show the world.

A dream came from my Grandma Elaine, the wife of my grandfather who had paid his debt to America through his military service. Grandma Elaine always had a face to show the world. She always would say, "I've got to go put on my face" and disappear in a bedroom or bathroom and complete her ritual of fresh make-up on her face. I didn't yet wear make-up as a teen and young adult; I guess I just stepped into the world unprepared. I don't think Grandma was superficial in her face products; it was a preserving ritual that painted her exterior with grace and dignity. She came to me in a dream and said, "I have to go put on my face." This mask of femininity was a badge of strength and confidence allowing her to put her best foot forward and arrive at an occasion prepared to behold and be seen.

After about a week of my drug-induced sleep, my father had enough. Up until this point, I was left alone to wallow.

Dad came to my bedroom, turned on the lights and opened the blinds in the lone window in the room.

"You can't sleep your life away," he said, his voice strong and commanding yet kind. "Get up; get dressed."

"What's the point?"

"Tara, you have to face the world."

"What's the use?"

"'Cause I said so," he said and left me alone with the intense light breaking through the darkness of the room and really my soul.

I dressed in jeans and a clean, baggy sweatshirt. The idea of taking a rejuvenating shower was too much to bear. I walked through the family room and found my dad dressed in a winter coat.

"Get your coat. We are going for a drive," he said, matter-of-factly.

"Daddd," I whined with tears at the brink.

"Just do it. I can't stand seeing you like this. So, the Army didn't work out. So what. You're a Meissner. You're not going to let that stop you. Now get your coat on."

Tears falling, nose running, and a lump growing in my throat, I did as I was told, somewhat grateful for the instructions.

We drove and drove that day, ending up at a meat market in another rural town to pick up that season's venison sausage. From there we drove into town to bring some to my aunt Gina Mae. She was surprised to see me. Looking back, I imagine, I was a smelly, fat, blob unworthy of love and kindness. She hugged me anyway.

"Tara, how are you? What happened?" she asked.

My dad hadn't told her about my ejection and rejection from the Army. I had to tell her myself.

"I'm such a loser," I choked. "I'm fat."

"You are not fat," Gina Mae said.

"No I am; it is stamped on my military records," I cried. "They kicked me out."

I went on to describe the entire horrific details: the Howard Johnson, the MEPS building, and the Greyhound bus. I didn't tell her about my week of over-the-counter induced sleep. She knew. Gina Mae understood. She let me spill my pain; she listened and didn't judge. I let the tears flow freely. I hugged her tight, oblivious to my odor.

On the way home, Dad and I rode silently. When we got home, he and I shared a plate of the venison sausage. I love venison sausage, and it was the first food I'd eaten since being rejected from the Army: It was delicious. I showered then, washing away a layer of pain and shame. I started to find my face. When I dressed in real clothes again, I found my way back to the kitchen.

"You have to find a job. Then you can get your own apartment. You will need health insurance. You have to move on."

I nodded, understanding manual labor was once again my only choice. I needed money, and manufacturing was the only place a young person with no skills who dropped out of college and was rejected by the military could find it.

A wool factory was advertising for a second shift job on a line. After a brief interview, they deemed me worthy of the position. A thin woman told me that she worked there for the exercise; I noticed I was doing the same work and it didn't make me any thinner. She had a permanent tan and sun-bleached blonde hair. Her work attire consisted of tight Harley-Davidson shirts and cut-off denim shorts. I wore loose-fitting clothing to hide my obesity.

I found this job to be symbolic to what I really wanted to do with my life. We each manned our own machine, generating bins of yarn in various stages of completion. There was the pulling room where the raw wool was fed into a machine to pull it into strands that would be balled. From there these thin threads were woven into thicker pieces at the machine I ran. As these balls of yarn went from station to station, they became thicker and were eventually ready to be shipped to other factories where socks and sweaters would be made. I was spending 40 afternoon and night hours a week spinning yarn, which made me consider that what I really wanted to do was become a writer. The idea that I would one day spin stories that others would read kept me going.

God's Promise

"Forgive me Father, for I have sinned. I can't remember my last confession," I told Father Tom sitting in the face-to-face confessional position.

His white collar tucked between black shirt and jacket spoke to his purity. I turned to him, unaware of where else to go. It was the only place to go. I sat in the wicker-backed chair. I looked past my blossoming belly to the floor between us. I fought back tears. I waited for my breath to return to me.

"Go on," Father Tom said.

I couldn't remember the rest of the confessional prescribed script. I looked up into his young face. He was 30 at best; I was 22. His hair was jet black – unlike the elderly, more intimidating priests of my youth. He could have a wife. He could have a girlfriend. Why did he choose this profession? I distracted myself with ponderings rather than getting on with my confession, which he could probably surmise with a glance at my naked left ring finger.

"Go on," he said again.

Somehow the words came tumbling out.

"I am pregnant and unmarried. I sinned," I said, my face red, my back slouched.

I didn't specifically mention the risky sex I had with a fellow I hardly knew. I didn't have to. The fact was I hadn't been in a committed relationship, but allowed myself to succumb to the passions of the flesh. I tarnished myself with a modern day scarlet letter. I wore the badge of impurity in my expanded uterus. Inside was an innocent child, who would be born without a father.

What the priest said, as I sobbed, surprised me. I was expecting a series of Hail Mary's and The Lord's Prayer. A rosary or two – or probably it would take hundreds to absolve this sin from me. Yet he didn't dole out any of those cliché penances.

"What I want you do is go out and be the best mother you can be," he told me.

That's it, I thought. I wiped my tears and nose with my sleeve as I wondered how I could possibly raise my child to the best of my ability in a broken home. The pregnancy, about seven months along, was already trying. The joyous moments like the ultrasounds, the flutter kicks, and hearing the heartbeat were hollow without someone there to share it. I had been abandoned at just three months gestation. I was living with my parents again in my childhood bedroom with floral paneling and a twin bed.

By this time, I had left the wool factory and was working second shift at a Greek restaurant as a waitress. The owner was kind. My co-workers were interesting. I liked some of the regulars. Some of the random customers, who happened by as a pit stop from the interstate, were rude. One burly gentleman asked me if I was German one night as I set down his plate of the daily special.

"Yah," I said. "How did you know?"

"I see you were playing that old German game," he said.

"Huh?"

"Hide the sausage," he laughed.

I am not sure if he was laughing at me or if he was laughing at his cleverness. I didn't laugh at his joke. I walked back to the prep station – head down.

I went to church weekly throughout the rest of my pregnancy. I knelt on swollen legs. I participated in the chanting and reciting and the singing. I felt the traditional Mass in my heart going beyond the motions. I felt the bowing and asking for forgiveness. I believed I was not worthy to receive the body of Christ. I hoped the communion ritual was correct: that I could only say the word and I would be healed. I wore a cross-shaped ring on my middle left finger. I clutched onto God and Jesus, because I had forsaken all other options. I didn't have friends around me; I had isolated myself. I was alone. Once more, I felt like I was a complete failure.

One week, I went to church and found that my beloved Father Tom – young and compassionate – had been transferred. We had talked briefly of my plans for baptism of the child. He had asked me to raise my child in the Faith. His replacement was another stereotypical old man with little understanding of accepting and forgiving modern transgressions. This new father denied me the chance to baptize my child, because he was born without a father. In order to have a baptism, I needed to bring the man who fathered my child to church with me. This man, who had shared my bed, refused to accompany me on what he considered a flawed religious tradition in a church other than the Lutheran he claimed to be.

The week after my son was born I brought the wrinkled bundle to church with my mom and dad at my side. Old man Father greeted us at the entrance and asked what I thought then was a stupid question.

"Where were you last week?"

"Um, I was in the hospital having a baby," I answered, ready to turn and walk back to the car.

"Well let's see him then," he said pulling the blanket free from his face. "What did you name the child?"

"Joseph James," I answered.

"Ah, very good. Old Testament and New," he said and gestured us inside the sanctuary.

Labor was a defeating blow. I fought through more than 30 hours of labor, arriving at the hospital Thursday evening and giving birth Saturday morning. It took several doses of pain medications and an ultimate epidural to get my body to relax and free the child from me. I cried. I asked God to kill us both. I hit a nurse. I couldn't let my body do its job. I couldn't relax. They tried having me take a hot shower. My sister Billie and my mom were in the room. They were of little comfort – really just reminders that there was a husband missing. There was a gloriously terrible thunderstorm Friday night into Saturday morning. The windows revealed a dark sky and the thunder booms shook the birthing room. Women came and went, all having their babies before me.

I delivered vaginally and the red, slimy mess of a child was placed on my stomach. Before I could react, exhausted with the ordeal, my mother had scooped up her new grandchild. A young grandmother at age 42, she swaddled him and comforted him before setting him at my breast.

"What is his name," the nurse asked me.

"Joseph James Meissner," I said.

Billie and my mother looked shocked. I was a little surprised myself. The name was not one that even made it into the running. "James" could be explained, because it is my mother's father's name. Yet, "Joseph" came right out of nowhere. Joseph was born in 1998 weighing 6 lbs, 9 ounces and measuring 21 inches. He had a good set of lungs and took to nursing without drama.

Friends and family, who I thought had forsaken me, came and brought gifts. Among these gifts was a Noah's Ark baby blanket, which was soft and fluffy. It became Joseph's favorite. That biblical story ends with a rainbow. I remembered my promise to God made in the confessional booth with young Father Tom. I thought of that priest's compassion and understanding every time I saw a rainbow, and I reminded myself to be the best mother I could.

First Diagnosis

I tried the pop psychology of self-esteem writers like Louise L. Hay and other so-called transforming idols like Oprah Winfrey. I was let down; I could not will the blues away. I knew enough to hide it, but I couldn't always hide it well. Depression was frequently with me.

The first treatment for depression came at age 22. This trip to a psychologist consisted of an hour assessment that I was mentally fine, but the doc concurred that my life stunk. He advised Prozac and sent me on my way. I'd like to protect the non quacks out there and say this type of thing doesn't happen, but it does. I was diagnosed with postpartum depression and referred to a medical doctor for a pill. This drive-through McMedicine – especially when concerning mental illness – was part of the problem with gaining credibility and proper treatment for a health problem.

When Joseph was six weeks old, I began working at a hardware warehouse, because unlike the restaurant it had the lure of much-needed health insurance. I had to let go of my childlike fantasy of marrying the right guy and raising a happy family as a stay-at-home mother. I had slept with the wrong guy and my son would grow up in a broken home. I wanted to do right by him. I vowed to give him the best life I could. I was determined to get a better apartment. I believed this situation was temporary. Believing it was just a stop on the journey and not a life sentence helped me cope. I thought I was better than my neighbors. I thought they were out of options. I still had my youth and a couple of years of college credits.

I didn't think I needed a psychologist, but rather a happy ending. I bought into the idea that my inability to control my moods was a personal weakness that could be overcome with mental aerobics. I thought if I exercised, ate better, and thought optimistically, I would not suffer from depression. I should be able to shower and feel content with the blessings that were around me: I had friends, I had a job, and I had the most beautiful baby imaginable. But I didn't feel this. I was disconnected from the reality of the positive things in my life. While there was nothing really wrong with my life, I did not feel like living it. My son kept me alive. But it was all I could do to wake up and shower each day. My thoughts were invaded with a constant, steady loop telling me I'd be better off dead. I realize now, it was outside my control. I thought then I should just muster more gumption to try harder.

Mom, who always did everything she could to make me happy, saw something more than life circumstance holding me back. She recognized a medical problem. She advised me to enter the world of psychiatry and psychotherapy – a world I would visit off and on throughout the decade leading up to my nervous breakdown. Mom gave me a friend's doctor's name and found his number for me, because her friend had benefitted from it. I ignored it. Persistent and loving, Mom made an appointment for me and told me to go.

I met this doctor feeling like a tossed out reject. I thought strong people didn't need help from psychotherapy. I thought this was a tremendous weakness on my part to need help from an outsider for something as innocent as a depressed mood. I told him my sob story. He recommended Prozac, which was supposed to make me feel better. He also told me I was too intelligent to be working in the job I had, but I didn't have any other option but to make the best of the situation I was in at the moment.

The Prozac made me fall into a slumber so deep I couldn't hear my child's cries in the night, so I started sleeping at my parent's house. I worked from 5 p.m. to 1 a.m. at the hardware warehouse. My parents babysat for Joseph after working their regular daytime jobs. Rather than going "home" to my apartment after my shift, I slept in my childhood bedroom on a twin bed with a playpen at its foot, until my son woke me in the early morning.

Sometimes, I stayed at my parents' house throughout the day, pulling out the Rubbermaid tote of baby toys the young grandparents had bought for their first grandson and spread them on their living room floor. I laid on the couch, often too heavy with misery to interact or play with him. I kept him safe, fed, and diapered. Occasionally, I smiled at him. He really was an alert, beautiful baby with blond ringlets. He was strong, rolled over early and had a good grip for toys. I read to him and read parenting magazines. I was determined to finally do something right. I really enjoyed being a mother more than anything else I had done up until that point. I was motivated to provide a life for him better than the one I grew up in; unfortunately, the circumstance of being an unmarried college dropout made for a less-than-ideal start. I tried hard not to focus on that and rather thought of him as a gift from God to give me purpose.

My parents' refrigerator tempted me with leftovers and other treats. I often ate until I felt nothingness. I never felt full, so I ate more. It was not hunger, but rather a void; I was trying to fill the void. I had unconditional love from my young son, who studied my face with his open, innocent blue eyes. He formed a little fist around my finger or thumb. He had no choice but to let me cover his forehead and face with kisses as I inhaled his fresh, baby smell.

Sometime before my parents came home from their day jobs, I packed him up and went "home" to the apartment complex. My neighbors were as down and out as I was, so I tried to make friends with them. I tried to tell myself it was like a college dorm. An outside door led to the two-story building. Each apartment bore its number on the door. Some people decorated their doors. It was winter, so there were wreaths. My apartment was on the second floor; its door didn't have a decoration displaying my personality. I tried to decorate my apartment to make it cheery. I tried to keep it clean.

My sink was filled with dirty dishes, but I always made sure the bottles were clean. Other remnants of meals eaten alone overflowed from both sides of the sink and sat on the cupboards. Eventually, I would grow so disgusted, I'd wash the dishes: a process that would take hours. I didn't own a TV. Instead of a couch, I had a fold-out futon. My bedroom was furnished with a nice set, handed down to me by my dead great-grandmother from my mother's side of the family.

My father was sympathetic to my dire living situation. He bought me a TV.

He said, "Tara, you have to have a television."

Like most men, Dad was practical. He did tangible things to provide me with cheer. He brought me venison and he bought me the TV. What he didn't say was how depressing my situation was. Dad couldn't stand by and do nothing as I existed in that state. I knew I was loved but had no idea how to give love back – I was empty. I was desperate. I hated my job; I didn't resent my son. He was the only thing that kept me alive. As depressing as this situation was, I wasn't suicidal: just unproductive and desperate. I remembered my failed attempt at college.

My job where I counted nuts, bolts and screws to ten and then weighed them on a scale was a big step down from my youthful aspirations of getting a college degree and then starting a respectable career, though I never focused long enough to figure out what exactly that career would be. I toyed with the idea of writing, just because I was repeatedly told I was good at it, but a job as a writer is not a very concrete idea or goal, so it was just a lofty ambition. I'd write a lot on an old word processor penning short stories and starting novel after novel. I also wrote scores of short poems, most of which were fairly depressing. I read a lot of Emily Dickinson and should have read more Robert Frost. As I spent eight hours a night mindlessly counting to ten, I daydreamed. Some of my co-workers were cognitively disabled or intellectually limited, as it is politically correctly called today. I was clearly functioning well below my capacity but lacked motivation to exert any energy to do anything else.

At the warehouse, my boss was a feisty 5-foot-tall woman with a mullet. Her tightly curled hair resulted from a permanent – I wondered if it was a home perm. She wore work boots and tight Levi's. I had health insurance, which made earning just over minimum wage worthwhile. I learned to drive a fork lift, yet I never got over the fact that a lady doesn't drive a fork lift. My Grandma Elaine had told me as a child two things about ladies: a lady never buys her own jewelry and a lady never eats everything on her plate. This was from a bona fide Rosie Riveter in her time.

Grandma had the gift of gab, a gift she passed through the generation gap; she told me I had it too. Teachers marked it excessive talking. But grandma, she knew that chatter – or at times monologues – were a blessing. She was a kind soul. The Lord filled her tiny frame. She saw beauty everywhere she chose to look in everything she could see. She saw beauty in me.

There was no question I wasn't very ladylike at this time of my life. I hauled heavy boxes. I counted to ten. I hated every moment of it. On the hierarchy of jobs, lifting heavy objects is the lowest rung. I was a bottom feeder. I didn't see a way up and out of this lowest class of society. I felt trapped.

We picked up a computer-generated sheet of orders to be filled. Some of the workers spit these forms out from the computer; I was not one of those "skilled" workers. I picked up a packing list from the bin and hopped on a fork lift. With hesitancy and visions of smashed workers reeling in my head from the safety videos I had to watch, I drove this heavy machine through the towering aisles. Each section of the labyrinth was coded. I found codes like YE12 or CB19 listed on the packing sheet, and another column told where the item was located. Thousands of parts – screws, bolts, nuts, nails, hinges – were stored in large cube boxes, some weighing as much as 80 pounds. That was one of the job requirements: an ability to lift up to 80 pounds. The quantity of pieces contained was listed on the box. After we subtracted what we took for our order, we were to cross off the quantity number and replace it. Not every employee could complete this simple math; the number of pieces listed was sometimes off a few screws.

Someone's life work was to organize and train us monkeys. Someone took this seriously. I was too proud to really care. It was hard to care about anything. I was depressed. I walked out of the job one night, fed up. I had no other job lined up. I walked away from my health insurance. I prayed something better would present itself. By the time I left, I had saved enough money to get a two-bedroom apartment – but without the steady paycheck, I was in danger of losing it. I left anyway.

Leaving was actually doing something. It forced me to change my circumstance. It forced me to "snap out of it." Later on, I returned to college and took an abnormal psychology class, where I learned that depression left untreated generally cleared up on its own after six to eight months. That is about how long I worked at the warehouse.

Bylines

The advice of the psychologists I saw off and on for depression was to set goals and work toward them. I did. I returned to work at the Greek restaurant after walking out on the warehouse gig. At least at the restaurant, I was able to interact with people. There were windows, too, unlike when I was trapped in a physically dark building with towering shelves of screws and nails. I enjoyed waitressing work enough. The best part was the part-time hours. I worked four to five nights a week for seven hours – generally from 4 to 11. I always had cash in my pocket and enough money to provide the basics. I lived with calculated risks of no auto or health insurance but kept food in the house and gas in the car, and paid the utility bills on time. I did not rely on my parents or public assistance. While I waited tables, I found a church-going family to watch my son in the evenings. Joseph and I spent the days together exploring the world. Life slipped into a comfortable, manageable phase.

As he approached his second birthday, I blended into the world as a single mom. I worked. I had my own apartment. I had dreams of becoming a writer. I taught him the basic toddler skills: please and thank you, numbers and letters, shapes and colors, potty training, and teeth brushing. He was healthy and happy, and adorable with naturally curly blond hair and eyes that would turn from blue to green. He wore pint-size, name-brand sneakers.

In due course, with some focused tenacity, I put together some writing samples and a resume and started to believe a career in journalism was within reach. In between the bad times, I did freelance for a county weekly and I did return to community college taking a few English and Communication classes. I was still well short of a bachelor's degree, and without a focused history of college, I didn't have an associate's degree or credentials of any sort. I was able to spin the experiences I did have with my opinion that I was talented and believed in myself. The catch phrase, "Do what you love and the money will follow" was taped to my wall where I saw it every day. I convinced myself I loved to write.

With a tax return, I bought a computer and was hooked up to the internet. Having decided to follow my dream, I was reading The Writer and Writers Digest magazines. I joined a statewide writers' association and a local writers' group. I didn't actually write much during this time, but I applied to numerous newspaper jobs, because the articles I was reading said this was a good way to get published and break into print.

The local press contacted me after my resume landed on the desk of Charlie Matthews. I later learned this man had skill but more importantly passion and compassion. He was in his 40s, had a wife and a couple of kids. At the time, all I knew was he was the news editor who happened to find my resume. He called me and offered me an assignment as a stringer. Elated, I accepted the challenge at once.

I had taken one journalism class and received a C grade for the course. I knew nothing about news writing, but I kept telling myself this was a writing position that could set me free from blue collar work.

While attending UW-Oshkosh, I took a philosophy class where we had to write a paper on theory. I wrote a piece titled "God's Rational Love," which explained why it was possible to believe something even though there was evidence to disprove that belief.

"All of you should be ashamed of yourself," the professor had addressed the class. "For college students, none of you know how to write a simple essay. I wonder how you made it through the entrance requirements."

I grew uncomfortable in my chair and slouched down. I was ashamed of myself for having slapped together my paper in about thirty minutes with a slight alcohol buzz.

"There are a few exceptions," he said, and turned to the desk.

The instructor made enough copies for the fifty-member class and handed out copies of a paper. As it came around, I realized it was my essay.

My little two-page essay illustrating a rational belief in God despite evidence against such a belief had won the heart of the professor.

"This is what writing should be," he said.

Another professor, of English Comp 101, also had given me some positive feedback for a research paper I wrote about rape.

"This is some of the best and most horrific writing I have experienced," he had scribbled on the cover page.

A professor in my Music Appreciation Class wrote in the margins of an essay test about Beethoven's Fifth Symphony, "Take your writing one step farther and recognize yourself as a genius."

I held to the memories of positive affirmation. I started to believe I had a vocation, a God-given talent, a gift for writing. As delusional as this may have been, it gave me hope and courage to continue to follow the path of my pen while raising Joseph.

I had sent out scores of resumes and these writing samples from college to small newspapers. When Charlie called me from the Herald Times Reporter and told me he had an assignment for me to write, I became hopeful that this would really be my break into the published word. That first assignment was to write a human interest feature story about a police science instructor at a nearby technical college. I did. I turned in a hard copy in person.

The receptionist at the newspaper office buzzed Mr. Mathews, who invited me right upstairs. I had Joseph with me, because I had no daytime childcare. I climbed the stairs carrying my son and setting him down at the top of the stairs. I followed the marked path to the newsroom, a noisy place with a maze of cubicles and a scanner blipping in the background. Charlie Mathews popped up from a cubicle like a rodent in the Whack-a-Mole arcade game when he heard me introduce myself to the receptionist in the office.

"Hi, Tara. Follow me," he said holding a manila folder. I did, holding Joseph's hand.

"I didn't realize you would want to meet with me," I said.

I handed him my article, which he read right in front me. I waited for the "not good enough" response, because I lacked self confidence. I had poured over the article trying to pick the lightning word rather than the lightning bug word like I had learned from reading advice of Mark Twain.

Minutes seemed like hours as I waited for Charlie to finish reading the piece.

"Number one, I'm going to publish this," Charlie said.

I tried not to act surprised.

"And number two, I'm going to pay you for it."

I gasped but tried to remain calm. Well, as calm as I could with an active toddler underfoot. By this time, Joseph was running all over the lunch room and had settled on turning a chair upside down and removing its screws. I leaped up to stop him.

"Boys will be boys," Charlie said.

"Okay, sorry I brought him," I said, embarrassed by my lack of professionalism.

"Don't worry about it," Charlie said.

The pay was $50 for the 1,000-word story. I later learned that the newspaper staff called all their articles "stories," a label I came to appreciate.

He reached into his manila folder, which contained scraps of papers describing story ideas, and gave me three more pieces to work on with deadlines. I took those assignments and went home to my apartment – but not before first stopping for ice cream with Joseph to celebrate my entrance into print. I could hardly wait to read my byline in the piece that would be published on Oct. 28, 2000. I thanked God in my thoughts and trusted His planned vocation for me. I was certain this path of writing would lead to success.

When I finished those stories, they kept giving me more and paying me for them. A couple of months later, the Herald Times Reporter hired a full timer to write the stories I had been doing. I was devastated; I had been foolish enough to think my freelance features would lead to a full-time job. The woman they hired was a college graduate with three years' experience writing for a daily paper. I was outmatched. The steady freelance assignments became more sporadic.

Then, in May, a man with 29 years with the paper was about to retire. The Herald Times Reporter Managing Editor Jerry Guy called me for an interview. He offered me a job as a beat reporter covering city government seven months after that first published feature article. I began working four days before my 25th birthday.

I worked at the daily newspaper with a then 16,000 circulation for five years. It was the closest place of belonging I ever felt. I was free to come and go as I pleased. I didn't have to sit at a desk for 40 straight hours. And my writing was being respected. I was getting calls for story assignments. For the first time in my life, I was doing something I considered respectable. Joseph was enrolled in a licensed daycare and I had health insurance. My life was really together.

Depression would visit me seasonally during this time, but I'd manage it with a prescription of Wellbutrin and for the most part this was the happiest five years of my life.

Bunch of Girls

People who knew me could see the disease more clearly than I could see it in myself. Throughout life, I pushed evidence of insanity beneath the surface, hiding it from view and recognition. I cherished my companion, Denial. A colleague at the newspaper once summed it up nicely: "That Tara, she's a great bunch of gals," Neil had said.

Neil commiserated with me about the stifling nature of the corporate policies handed down to the local staffers from the media conglomerate Gannett Industries. Our opinion was these policies seemed intrusive and contradictory to the appeal of a small-town press; the Mc-management and "cooperate culture exercises" thwarted our efforts to capture feature and news stories in a way specific to the community where we lived.

Gannett instructed us to "NICHE it," which is an acronym standing for News, Impact, Context, and Human Element. The idea was to use this formula to include those items in the first five paragraphs. While this is not such a bad idea, the reasoning was marred. The technique was designed so the copy desk could chop off the story after the first five graphs and the reader would still understand the news based on the nuggets captures in the leading sentences. However, in-depth, developed stories were discouraged as an approach, responding to the shrinking news hole. Ironically, in my opinion, this approach contributed to the decline in readership, which meant a decline in advertising dollars.

Neil and I often escaped cubicle land with a lunch or coffee break. Sometimes my future husband, Mike, would join us. One day, the three of us decided to have lunch at the greasy spoon within walking distance of the newspaper office.

We all ordered. Then the conversation turned to the group's commonality: me. Mike told Neil how we met. Neil told Mike about some of our adventures after hours at our favorite bars. Neil warned Mike that I was a lot to handle. He was kind enough not to mention my rage, erratic moods, and uneven temperament in detail.

Neil then told Mike the line which would haunt me: "That Tara, she's a great bunch of girls."

If this comment fazed Mike, he didn't show it. He chuckled with the pair of us. We made light of its meaning – another technique I used repeatedly to cope with the consequences of the often present symptoms of my at-the-time nameless mental illness. Of course, I didn't consider myself having a mental illness at that time; I just thought I struggled with the blues and needed to try harder to be happy. I felt genuine happiness or contentedness was just outside my grasp. Sometimes it seemed so out of reach I entertained suicide, but the grace of God saved me from attempting that. I also thought everyone felt depressed like I did. I wouldn't, at that time, use the word depression in a clinical sense. Even though I took medication for it, I still didn't recognize it as a medical problem. I sometimes didn't go to the doctor when I felt depressed, but rather stopped at the Natural Market to purchase St. John's Wort, a natural supplement that did combat the blues enough to keep me functioning.

Neil's comment that day gave me pause and made me wonder if I came across as schizophrenic. I wondered – and not for the first time in my life – if there was something beyond my control that plagued my attempts at a consistently productive life.

I had often feared this possibility, but as Neil said it at lunch, I laughed it off and said something to pooh-pooh the comment. I vowed to try harder to control my emotions and to act more calm and steady at work and, really, in all corners of my life. While Neil's assessment of me as a "bunch of girls" held some truth, I did not have a personality-splitting disorder. My emotions seesawed with the slightest of modifications in routine. I could be happy, then suddenly, an innocent incident could trigger a response completely inappropriate for the occasion. My perception of reality was often through a pessimistic lens. I felt doomed, and as a result, debilitating depression came and went through the years. I also felt happy, though up until this point, I would not classify any of my behavior as manic.

Whacked Thyroid

The breast pump went flying through the living room and into the dining room where my husband Mike was standing. Unfortunately, it didn't hit him. I wanted him to hurt, like I was. I wanted him to share the shame, pain, and frustration that ate at my body. I had the cracked nipples that stung when they hit fabric as soft as a cotton bra, a bleeding uterus that soaked pad after pad and spilled onto the sides of my panties, and pain in my back — that damn constant pain.

I had been sitting on the corner of the couch trying to figure out how to juggle the suction cups affixed to four-ounce bottles and the tubes that ran to the machine that was powered through an outlet behind me. The cords and tubes tied around me. I was not wearing a shirt; I was not even wearing a bra. I was slouched and trying to "relax" attached to this contraption. The stretch marks across my abdomen screamed at the trauma of the birthing process. I was exposed completely to Mike in all my glorious hideousness. My infant son was napping upstairs. I had to pump, because my twelve-week maternity leave was soon to expire and I needed to build up a supply of breast milk for the day care.

I felt Mike staring at me while I tried to get the milk to come. I couldn't do it. I couldn't pump eleven ounces at a time like other women reportedly did. I couldn't even get an ounce to come and that was after thirty minutes of suction from both sides.

I couldn't. Not with him watching me like that. In hindsight, he was probably just curious as to how the damn thing worked. He stood in the next room just watching me. Not saying a word. I cursed him for not being able to help me. I felt sweat dripping down my back. I had a knot in my stomach.

In a twisted justification I thought he had it coming, I hurled that damn pump across the room aiming for his smirking face. Maybe he wasn't smirking. Maybe there wasn't anywhere else to go in our smallish two-bedroom house. I should have tried to pump with privacy in a dimly lit room where I could relax.

When the pump hurled through the room, Mike screamed at me. "What are you doing?"

"What was that for?"

I don't know what I replied. I don't remember. I know there were tears and insults and probably a long monologue about how he deserved to be on the other side of my rage. Luckily my older son Joseph, then age 7, was at school and our newborn son, Thomas, was napping.

Postpartum depression came back after Thomas was born, but with a lot more rage and tears than when it came before with Joseph. Maybe having a husband made it different. He was there to hold and diaper Thomas. I had the luxury of wallowing, even as Mike probably thought he was pampering me, his presence, love, and support enabled me to sink into a depression that was far more severe than anything I had experienced to this point. Every time I bent into my baby's bassinet and reached for him, my back screamed in pain. The joints in my spine throbbed. But it wasn't just the physical pain. It was the fact that I didn't feel connected to him in the way a mother should love her infant.

His birth was much easier physically and emotionally than Joseph's. My water broke while I was at a rummage sale on a Friday evening. We went to the hospital around midnight and he was born with the ease of an epidural around 8 a.m.

Saturday morning. The hospital had a great view of Lake Michigan and I joyfully accepted visitors and well wishers. Mike was the picture of a proud father and was a great source of comfort in the birthing room.

The thought of returning to work created a stressful anxiety in me. I began to disappear. I was no longer a happy newlywed with another beautiful baby. Mike, ever the champion, woke up with the baby, changed his diaper and set him at my breast while I lay in bed nearly catatonic, motionless, and let the baby suckle. Then I turned over to my other side and did the same.

During the day, I watched shitty, daytime television. Thomas was a good baby. He didn't cry much. Family and friends would stop by and remark how much they liked his hair and his smile. He was born with a full head of black curly hair. I see now from the pictures that he really was a beautiful baby. My perception was distorted. I was trapped in another state of postpartum depression. My mind reeled with images of loading up the kids and driving off the north-side pier into Lake Michigan. I didn't tell anyone at that time, but I knew depression was consuming me again.

But Mike was there. He shouldered the demands: he made the meals, cleaned up the house, bought the groceries and the diapers, and paid attention to Joseph's school schedule. He let me sleep whenever he was home, and he was home a lot. I didn't shower most days; I wore the same clothes day after day. All I had to do was feed the baby, from my breast. All good moms breastfed, formula was bad – only bad moms fed their infants formula. There was an expectation. I was a good mom, damn it. I was doing the best I could.

It wasn't the depression that debilitated me enough to seek help. It was the back pain that crippled me enough to seek out an internist. I was afraid I had rheumatoid arthritis, just like my mother. I couldn't stand up straight.

I went to a medical doctor and told her all about the back pain. How it was worse in the morning. How it was impossible to bend. How it was hard to hold my baby. I told her nothing of the thoughts of killing myself and my children. I told her nothing of my excessive sleeping and lack of showering. I put on a good show that day. Even put on a tad of make-up: eyeliner, mascara and some gloss for my lips.

She listened to my story, considered the family history, and questioned my weight and how long it was a problem.

"Have you ever been treated for a thyroid imbalance?" she asked.

"No. But my aunt, who owns a vitamin store, once told me she thought my thyroid was off," I said.

"Well, I am going to take a blood sample for that. Sometimes thyroid problems can cause joint pain. We just want to rule everything out," she said.

I gave some blood.

The results came back confirming hypothyroidism. Not arthritis. I began taking Synthroid, a synthetic hormone replacement. The back pain went away. Slowly so did my feelings of anger and depression. Without the physical pain, everything was easier to deal with. I gave up the nursing, though. Mike assured me it was okay. We started stocking the cupboards with formula when Thomas was four months old. I felt the hypothyroidism could explain my lifetime of mood instability. I thought with the hormone therapy, I could keep depression and moodiness at bay. For a while that worked.

PART TWO: THE BREAK

Holy Week (March 28 – April 4, 2010)

VOICES

For some time, I had been telling Mike I was functioning beyond capacity, but he didn't believe me. A person could juggle a part-time work schedule, a handful of online classes, and a trio of sons.

"Lots of women do it; you can too," my husband reassured me every time I complained.

I, however, could not.

It's funny what will harm us. For me it was dancing naked, meeting Jesus Christ, and party planning with Ellen DeGeneres. On Palm Sunday, the damage started, but the cause was present long before then: perhaps at my birth and perhaps even from generations prior.

It was one of the finest springs in recent history. The gray slush of a gradual spring didn't appear, or if it did, I hadn't noticed. The days were sunny with mild temperatures. It was as if winter gave way to the transformative season and never looked back. Without the typical ping-ponging from sunny skies to rainy chills to late-season flurries, the weather just kept getting better as spring emerged strong with no chance of a lingering winter guest. The season was beautiful with early robin sightings, greening lawns, and budding trees. In contrast of dreary brown grass and muddy yards found during a typical Wisconsin spring, tulips and daffodils bloomed that March throughout the neighborhood.

I was letting my hair grow long again. My three sons — Joseph, 11, Thomas, 4, and Alex, 2 — all had curly hair. When I freed my hair from its tight bun, it cascaded to my shoulders with natural, shampoo-commercial waves. Most people didn't realize I had curly hair, because I hid it. When they asked where the boys got their curls, I usually just said, "from my husband." It was my involuntary practice to gently dismiss my good qualities and find ways to subtly put myself down. But that spring was different. I didn't put myself down; instead I was a star craving spotlight and recognition.

I had moved on from the job at the newspaper and was working twenty hours a week as a transportation coordinator; I drove fifty freeway miles twice a week and worked the third day from home. It was designed as the often sought after, perfect work-family balance; I even had a nanny come to my home on the days I traveled to the office. I was completing my final semester of my once-neglected bachelor degree with a 3.9 GPA. I took a body sculpt class at the Y twice a week. Despite the fact that my scale registered 180 pounds and I could only run three minutes before having to walk to catch my breath, I was confident I would complete the Bellin Hospital 10K Benefit Run in June. I had quit smoking in November and was feeling pretty damn good about pretty much everything in my life. Mike told me I looked like an actual fitness buff in my running tights carrying my iPod Nano on a bicep band. I listened to The Indigo Girls mostly.

I felt so good in fact, I didn't think I even needed my husband. I thought we were a bit of an odd couple and that we didn't have anything in common past the kids and our shared love of books. I also felt he didn't like me or appreciate me. My perceptions were:

He's boring. I'm sexy.

He's calm. I'm active.

He's a loner. I'm a people person.

He's stagnant. I'm going places.

He's not a church person. I'm Catholic.

Early on in the marriage, I was quick to concede the Catholic faith and after trying other Christian congregations, we fell out of the habit of church service of any type. I thought then a woman was to follow her husband's lead. Over time, his sense of peace outside the confines of strict tradition bothered me. I felt religion was a major missing piece in our family. He didn't seem to care.

So, it wasn't unusual that we hadn't been to church to get a palm, despite it being a Holy Day of obligation. The beginning of Holy Week was on my mind, though, and I felt slightly guilty for missing the rituals of the week leading up to Easter Sunday. Easter always had been my favorite holiday, even more than New Years or my birthday or the start of school year; the resurrection of Christ was the ultimate opportunity to wash away past transgressions and begin fresh with the best of intentions for a respectable life. The discussion (pronounced argument) as to whether or not we should go to Mass didn't happen, because we weren't home.

Mike and I had spent the weekend at the state capitol watching my oldest son participate at a youth wrestling tournament. When we arrived home from Mad Town, an affectionate name many Wisconsinites dub Madison, Wisconsin, I felt outstanding. I was proud of my son and confident beyond measure, but I also hadn't slept all weekend. It was the norm for the parents to party at the hotel the evening after the two-day tournament ended. A potluck was thrown together and the coach ordered pizzas. I brought cucumbers, carrots, tomatoes, broccoli, and peppers. Everyone else brought junk food.

After two days of vendor food, I was pretty happy to provide fresh vegetables. I told the parents that they should eat more vegetables and take their wagon to their neighborhood grocery store to buy produce. I also told my friend with five sons she was a mother duck and her husband was a cool duck whose feathers never got ruffled. The party continued into the wee morning hours, many parents drinking, though I kept the same can of beer with me all night not really drinking. When Mike and Joseph grabbed a few hours of sleep, I stayed still and awake waiting for them to stir in the morning.

Still, I didn't feel at all tired when we returned to Manitowoc in the late afternoon Sunday. We had left our two younger sons at a friend's house for the weekend. Dan and Jane lived around the corner from us, so we walked through a neighbor's yard to arrive at their back porch. Dan answered the door and gestured for us to come inside; we stepped inside leaving our shoes at the door.

"How'd you do at the tournament?" Jane asked Joseph in her kitchen.

"Uh, I took sixth," he said.

"That's great," Jane said knowing there were sixteen other wrestlers in his age and weight bracket at the state tournament who had advanced from larger brackets at eight regional sites.

As she continued to talk with Joseph about his weekend, our younger boys tackled Mike as he tried to gather their things from the kitchen table. I walked farther in the house to the living room and found Dan sitting on the corner of his couch. The living room furniture was arranged in a circle with an area rug placed in the middle.

"You rearranged your furniture," I said.

"Yep," he responded.

I impulsively hopped on and off the rug in the circle placed before me. The round shape informed me something good was inside its circumference. This circle reminded me of the Alliant Energy Center, where Joseph had wrestled, which was fashioned like a coliseum, another circle of goodness. The wrestling matches had taken place at the center stage with rows of spectator seats spiraling out three stories. This memory, coupled with the talking furniture ring, reinforced an idea that the circle represented wholeness, goodness, completeness.

"Come into the good life," the circle tempted me.

As I hopped, I felt the circle was a sign showing me the way to righteousness. I believed the circle. I believed Dan understood what was taking place.

"Can I come into your circle?" I asked Dan as I continued to hop in and out of the ring at its summons to do so.

"Sure," he said.

Dan is a laidback guy who works in IT for a large, local company. He isn't overly social or gregarious usually, and that day wasn't an exception. Dan just sat reading the newspaper. I didn't feel odd as I jumped on and off his rug. I don't, as a matter of course, experience shapes provoking me to jump inside, but I didn't tell Dan this. I assumed he already knew about the circle and its wholeness and had known all along, which was why he chose to place his furniture that way.

Jumping into the center of the room, to me, was entering the core of Christianity. I thought I was gaining acceptance to the world of believers.

"Have you been here the whole time?" I asked Dan, wondering if he was at the heart of Christianity.

He nodded.

It almost didn't make sense that he was a Christian. Dan and Jane were not evangelical; they had never talked scripture with me. As far as I knew, they didn't attend worship services of any type. Yet their daughter was named Sarah with an "h" — a good, strong biblical name. I stood in the circle, pleased with my discovery that Christians are indeed silent in their work for the Lord, letting Jesus work through them in a subtle way that only other Christians can recognize. I was certain Christ was revealing this truth to me using the circle and my gentle friend as a vessel to show me this sign on a path to righteousness.

Faith in the Father, Son, and Holy Spirit was reasonable, though this theology I practiced never completely held my conviction. Throughout my life, I loosely held onto the Catholic traditions as an insurance policy against Satan. Regarding the legitimacy of religion, the power of doubt always cast shadows in the little light of mine. I did feel I owed it to my children to pass down the teachings of The Church, but it felt unnatural and forced to me.

"Whole time, huh, Dan?" I asked, for confirmation of my internal monologue.

I imagined that Dan, who was somewhat quiet in his mannerisms, was confident in his beliefs and was conditioned to be welcoming to new believers. In that moment, I saw his friendship as the work of a Christian revealing in a patient way the kindness of genuine believers.

"Whole time," he agreed, although he probably meant he was in his house the whole time, not in the Christian flock.

Mosaic

Later on Palm Sunday, the boys were settled into watching cartoons on our ridiculously large flat screen TV. Mike and Joseph wanted it; I had little choice, but the noise of a TV often bothered me. I preferred quiet. I hated the TV and the glazing effect it had on my family.

I stared out the window with an incredible need for calm and stillness. I tried to block out the noise of the television, but at the same time was grateful for the pacifying effect it had on our boys. I sat on the couch, which was placed alongside our three front windows, with my back to the TV and, really, to the entire family.

I contemplated the meaning of life and begged my family for silence. This selfish moment stretched into hours, but I had no concept of time other than the new cartoons that kept coming on after the music of the credits echoed in the background. I screamed at my husband and children when their innocent noise interrupted my concentration and introspection. I knew, even in that moment, that at some level I was losing it. I felt if I could just relax, I could regain stability.

We had decorated those windows with colorful Easter jelly-like, puffy clings. Through the glass I noticed the bakery across the street — it was one of those old-fashioned bakeries you don't see often anymore. It was closed on Sundays, but in the morning the bakery would have fresh bread, iced donuts, cookies, and cakes. I marveled at the beauty of living in its proximity, the preserved slice of better life from history. As I gazed out the window, I mindlessly pulled the clings off and ripped them into pieces. I reaffixed these pieces into a mosaic shape jumbling the colors. I just ripped and placed the colored gels among one another, piecing together a picture. I only saw the pieces of the mosaic and the evenly-spaced slivers of exposed glass between them. I couldn't see what they became.

This tearing and placing and staring took place silently amidst the chaos of a home with our three boys and my confused husband. Mike probably was wondering why I was nearly catatonic and still rather than helping him unpack from our long weekend in the state capitol, yet he indulged me. I convinced him I needed to unwind. He just paced, occasionally looked down on me, and when I wouldn't divert my attention from the window, he mumbled under his breath. I noticed this only peripherally, too intent on myself to pay him any attention.

While I stared out the window, I dismissed Mike's suggestion to eat. I did not move. I screamed. I demanded silence. I sat and stared. I explained I needed ONE MORE MINUTE. Hours must have passed. I may have appeared crazy to them, but it seemed rational to want to sit and stare outside and create an arrangement of ripped up pieces on the window pane. I felt I deserved some peace and quiet after the long weekend. I needed some "me" time to gear up for Spring Break that week. The older boys were off school for Holy week, even though they did not attend religious schools.

"What are you doing?" Mike asked more than once.

Each time, I considered an answer but couldn't find a worthy reply. It seemed so obvious to me: I was relaxing, trying to grasp clarity. I wondered what he could not see, could not understand.

He shook his head and left me alone, permitting me further introspection as he unpacked, quieted the children, and tucked them into their beds.

Being a writer who has taken up the work seriously and not seriously off and on throughout my life, I had more than a few half-finished novels sitting in various forms — floppy disks, printed word processor pages, thumb drives, and notebooks. As I sat at the window, I became convinced I was on the cusp of a great understanding of the meaning of life. I was certain life's mysteries were about to be unfolded before me. I needed more time to sit and contemplate and wait for the inspiration to take hold within my mind, and then transcribe these findings. I had been writing frantically the past several weeks, working on a literary novel that examined the seven sacraments of the Catholic Church.

After what must have been hours of sitting still, I got a zing of energy: I reached an epiphany. I grabbed the dot-matrix paper roll left over from the days of spooled printers and spread the relic pages across the dining room table. I scribbled single words and clustered them with others. I solved a mystery. I realized my purpose on this earth was to meditate to seek the truth and then capture it to leave to generations present and future. I used colored pencils of different hues to code the message esoterically, so no one could steal my work. I amazed myself with the wisdom that came to me. I was frantic, I could not stop. I unlocked a door within myself, and I was afraid the time of this insight would expire without warning.

I started to hear Jesus then. He told me at midnight the fountain of knowledge would end. I had to document all of this information quickly. The Lord had chosen to share His wisdom with me. I had to write it all down, shorthand.

I understood then that I was a prophet. I had to share the knowledge that came to me with the world. I wrote and drew arcs and made heavy concentric circles around key clues of insight. I drew rainbows with the equal signs connecting it to the word promise. I wrote heavy underlines emphasizing the number five and the word family. These were the revelations that came to me following my hours of contemplative searching. These were the ideas that demanded transcription.

I was beyond a bit eccentric, I was losing control. Yet I accepted this passage, honored to have been chosen as a vehicle of the Lord to spread His message. I was sure I was at the cusp of writing the next great American novel, a literary work that would change history.

"What are you doing?" my husband asked again.

Oh, the simple-minded, mortal man, he couldn't possibly know. He couldn't understand. I had to color and code the work. I dismissed him with a flip of my hand.

Fracture

Eventually, Mike convinced me to go to bed. He fell asleep quickly, but I stayed awake. I ran up and down the stairs making a lot of noise. I was naked. I can't say for sure what time it was, but I know it was sometime after I received the wisdom from Christ.

"Go to sleep. Go to sleep, Tara," Mike said to me with his heavy, angry footsteps echoing down the stairs.

I couldn't obey him and go to sleep; there was too much commotion around me. I repeatedly mounted the stairs and tried again to sleep. We had a great master suite at that house. The boys had rooms downstairs, and the entire upstairs was ours. The bedroom had a skylight over our bed and a walk-in cedar lined closet. In the hallway was a dormered alcove where I set up my home office. The tiled bathroom had a walk-in shower with two shower heads.

Each time I laid down in our bed and heard Mike's breath begin to relax into slumber, the messages would come. I tried to shield myself by pulling our heavy maroon comforter to my chin. I inhaled the familiar scent of our night sweat mixed with fabric softener.

Yet, the inability to sleep was outside my control. I couldn't sleep, because a message kept taunting me, tempting me to leave. Something invaded my mind and manifested in what must have looked like insomnia.

After 72 hours of straight wakefulness, I began to realize something other than me was keeping me awake. I had believed Yoga had helped me stay awake over the weekend, because I would refresh with a Salamba Sarvangasana shoulder stand pose. When I felt tired, I'd lie down and slowly swing the weight of my back, butt, and legs to rest upon my shoulders thus positioning my legs perpendicular to the floor with the bottom of my feet parallel to the ceiling. I'd hold this pose for 30 minutes, because an instructor had told our Tuesday morning yoga class doing so would give the body the same benefit as sleeping for four hours. A preposterous notion, but remarkably, I convinced myself it was true.

After three days of this practice, staying awake was no longer a perceived choice but rather a state of being in which I was trapped. The physical stress of not sleeping for days was cracking my brain, leaving room for intruders to drop anchor. Jesus Christ was trying to talk to me. Frightened, I ran down the stairs again and muttered incoherently.

Mike followed me downstairs.

"Tara, you aren't making any sense. I can't understand what you're saying."

"You need to sleep," he said, and this time he physically embraced me as we climbed the stairs and he tucked me into bed. He kept muttering "you're okay" and "you just need to sleep."

I may have slept or at least rested enough for the voices to return. A message returned repeatedly.

I couldn't put the nonsense polluting my brain into a tidy box to take out later to explore or lock away for good. Something crashed through the protective walls of self, and there was nothing Mike or I could have done on our own to stop its preset course.

I wanted peace from the loops of turmoil that unspooled from my mind. I desired refuge, but the thing is as I lay in my bed willing myself to a place of stillness while trying to fall asleep, I received the notice telling me I should die that night.

A message of a plan of a death countdown came repeatedly each time stronger and clearer than the last. The plan was an auditory hallucination, but I didn't know that then. I believed the plan and therefore accepted completely the summons from beyond to break consciousness.

I surrendered to what I now know was psychosis and let it take its course. But really, I had no choice but to abandon life and pray that I would be okay. There was little sight of earth any longer. I was detached from my body, harshly, to a foreign place vaguely logical based on distortions of Christian teachings. I was ensnared alone in a world that didn't exist outside my mind. These events were so absurd, my husband was inadequately prepared to catch me as he and my children witnessed a woman — who looked very much like the wife and mother they loved — acting as if possessed. I later learned my eyes were unfocused, dancing wildly.

But I heard the voice of Jesus Christ! He had my complete attention. His message looped convincingly as the Word of God. He told me my number was up and it was time for me to decide to die. He told me I was born with free will, and I alone needed to decide if I would die to live with him eternally, or if I would ignore His message and live as a nonbeliever.

"There is an elaborate plan of the world. Death is certain for everyone," Jesus said. "Tonight I share with you the secrets of this plan. Each person receives advance notice when their number is nearing. It is up to each person to decide to trust me and Christianity. It is up to each person to have faith strong enough to die and trust me to reach eternal life."

Jesus continued, "You are number three in the plan. If you don't choose to die, your husband will face the same decision tomorrow night; Mike is number two."

"If each of you chose to live on your respective turns Al Neuharth will die. The list ends there. Mr. Neuharth will have no choice; he will die at your selfish hands. One of you must die to save the other on the countdown list. Many have gone before you over the past 33 years of your life. Some died and many selected to live. This is the list that lays before you. This is your choice. You can save the other names on the list. If you decide to die, then they will get slotted back into my deck, but tonight is the night you have to come to a decision."

"Do you believe I am real?" Jesus asked.

I did. He was clearly with me. I couldn't see Him, but I sensed his presence. I couldn't believe what He was asking of me. I tossed and turned as I considered the pair of names following mine on the list. I willed the message to stop, but it persisted. I was not ready to die, but I was morally plagued with indecision. I felt urgency; if I waited too long it meant I selected to live and would force the decision onto my husband. I didn't want Mike to suffer and die, but Al Neuharth's death was worth considering. However, this final name depended on Mike also selecting to live. I reasoned Mike might have enough courage to leave this world and our family to cross into immortality. I weighed the scenarios in my head, unable to escape my mind.

I wondered what Mike would decide if I forced that torment on him. I was under attack. I cried at the idea of leaving my family behind. Physically, I felt hot. I wanted to be free of the covers since I felt sweat covering me. I brainstormed a way to live and have Mike live as well. Yet, this meant Al Neuharth would die at our hands. I knew Al Neuharth founded Gannett's flagship paper the USA Today. I had once worked for a rinky-dink Gannett paper swallowed up by the media conglomerate, until I left that job in a ray of self-righteousness because I believed I was far too creative to conform to corporate culture.

Advanced in age, Mr. Neuharth had lived a full and productive life filled with great accomplishments. Maybe it was his time, I considered. Jesus, of course, ever omniscient, knew what I ultimately would decide; his all-knowing presence gnawed at me. Jesus just nonchalantly waited for me at the foot of my bed to process the choice before me. This infuriated me. I cursed Him for making me decide — I thought He was supposed to be kind and loving and guiding. I was pissed. Then I reasoned that people were responsible for the stories I knew of Jesus and that here he was IN MY ROOM and I had to, at minimum, show him some respect.

Forcing death on Neuharth, whom I have held responsible for the declining quality of print journalism, would have made me a murderer. In the information age of online readers, the traditional product of a newspaper packed with local news and small-business advertising delivered by the neighborhood kid on a bicycle was heading toward extinction. My friends and former colleagues were losing their jobs. Meanwhile, Neuharth, I imagined, was country-clubbing it somewhere in Florida. It was easy to hate this man, who may well be a fine man. It was easy to loathe him for his success, because of the casualties. Was this the fault of Gannett's McMedia approach to news delivery or just the changing landscape of journalism in general? Was Neuharth responsible? I allowed myself to think I could save newspapers if I killed Neuharth by deciding to live.

I remembered reading *The Chain Gang: One Newspaper Versus the Gannett Empire* by Richard McCord. This book explored the questionable ethics of Gannett Industries and one newspaper in Green Bay, Wisconsin, that held on to compete against the growing franchise. I blamed Neuharth for the ethical decline of the largest newspaper chain in the country. When I started as a reporter, there was a clear division between news and advertising. Over time, that line blurred. Money talked. Someone from advertising once told me he paid my salary.

"Check the front page. I'm pretty sure you'll find my name. People are buying what I'm writing," I remembered having said smugly, naively.

Yet I couldn't in good conscience make myself responsible for Neuharth's death — or worse, Mike's.

While the idea of leaving Mike was inconceivable, the idea of him selecting death and leaving me was unbearable. I knew that I couldn't have him die. To spare him even the choice, I decided to sacrifice my life to save Mike and Neuharth. Ultimately, I placed my trust in Jesus and His plan for me in the afterlife. The only way to die was in my sleep, so I closed my eyes and prayed for guidance the only way I knew how. Consistent with the teachings of the book of Luke 11:2-4, I prayed, "Our Father which art in heaven, Hallowed be thy name ..."

I muttered the Lord's Prayer until it became a rhythmic combination of sounds — no longer words. These sounds became a comfortable hum uttered to shelter myself from the mental noise that was all around me. I fell into a slumber, which ultimately meant I was awaiting my rebirth with Christ. I tried to make peace with my decision by willing Jesus to stay with me and make my transition to the afterlife endurable.

The ramifications of my choice disrupted my passage. I woke several times throughout the night in a panic. I was frightened. I thought I was too young to die at age 33. I thought of all I would have to leave behind.

"It is all part of my plan," Jesus assured me.

"You are not alone," I was told. "In fact, all the Taras are facing this choice tonight, and each of them has another number in my plan."

Jesus complicated his message then. He had to be sure I would selflessly choose to die to save my husband from the decision and Neuharth from a fatal fate. Then he told me all the Taras were facing their own countdown lists at this same time. Jesus, omnipresent, was rolling out this scenario to each Tara living in the world. All the Taras were on the choose-to-live-or-die list. Some Taras had higher numbers. My number was so low at 3, because I had spent so much of my life wishy-washy rather than having a solid conviction and faith in Jesus Christ as the Savior of mankind.

Jesus told me if every Tara decided to die, the world would end. One had to select life, because the Taras were born to love and protect the earth.

"If every Tara decides to the die tonight, the earth will face Armageddon," Christ revealed. "You have to let the Taras know that you have selected death and convince at least one other to select life."

Since I already decided to die to save my husband and Neuharth, I had to find a way to save the earth before I could cross over to eternity. I had to take the risk of dying and entrust some other Tara to forgo death and choose to live. I was scared. I wanted my children to be okay and live on a healthy and sustainable earth. I was afraid of destroying all of mankind.

To counteract my fears, I logged onto Facebook to recruit some help. I quietly worked on the computer so not to wake Mike. I was feeling somewhat calm and focused at this point: I knew what I had to do. I typed hundreds of status updates to my 200 "friends." About twenty of them were "online" in the middle of the night. I hoped to reach a Tara: my friend's list had five Taras. None of them were showing up online, so I could only hope that someone would alert them. Meanwhile, I sent out short little clips:

"Calling all Taras"

"The"
"End"
"I"
"Choose"
"Death"
"The earth remains"
"Jesus lives"
"Calling all Taras"
"Taking one for the team"
"Team man"
"Mankind"
"Women too"

There were hundreds of these. Afflicted with torment, I made the frantic loose associations logical in my mind and hopefully in the mind of another believer who would understand the Word of God in this code.

In the midst of this insanity, my actions were temporarily calm and rational. I believed this alerting system was expected of me, and that I was being obedient to the Savior. I knew it was my responsibility to save the world. I had to communicate as a prophet of Christ. I had to give testament to His life to recruit believers. I was chosen to receive first-hand knowledge and had a responsibility to spread the Word of God.

I returned to bed and once again recited the Lord's Prayer in a quiet chant. I confirmed my decision to die that night. I cloaked myself with recitation to shield the chaos. I used the dead man's yoga pose to become still on my back with my arms by my side and legs straight. I used this pose as a relaxation tool and forced myself to actually die in my sleep.

My passage was again interrupted as Jesus returned.

"You have to alert the children," He said.

"Wake Joseph and tell him to enlist his friends to start to rebuild the world. While you sleep and die, the entire world will be rebuilt. You will walk among the believers. You are going to be rewarded for the morally sound decisions you have made. You selflessly decided to trust in me and die, and as a result you will save the earth. But I need you to enlist the children. They know this day is coming. They are waiting for it. Tell Joseph you received the message."

I understood that my 11-year-old boy and his friends could use their hand-held electronic devices to reconstruct the world. Those children always knew more than the adults did, I chuckled. At the wrestling tournament, my oldest son and his friends played a hand-slapping game at the hotel.

One of the mothers had said, "Look, it is like a Sunday School game."

I grabbed hold of that memory, which I recognized as a planted sign from God, an indicator that God and Jesus and church are the true paths to eternity.

I ran down the stairs urgently, loud, and heavy. I jolted my oldest son awake with a violent shake.

"JOSEPH. JOSEPH. WAKE UP," I said with panic in my voice.

"I received the message," I continued, fully expecting him to know what I meant.

Joseph groaned heavy with sleep, but was rubbing his eyes and looking around.

"You have to alert the children," I said. "Joseph, are you listening? Dewey, he's the leader. Is he one of your Facebook friends?

"What?" he said. "Mom what are you talking about it?"

"THE WORLD. It's Ending. You have to Save it. TODAY, you have to start the rebuild. I am dying tonight."

"MOM, what are you talking about?" Joseph said as he cried.

"Joseph, do you understand?"

Mike came down the stairs seeming more pissed than concerned.

Joseph seemed confused and scared.

Mike asked me, "What are you DOING? GO TO SLEEP!"

I wanted to obey and have peace. I wanted to go to sleep. I wished Mike understood what was happening. I felt so alone. I told him of The Plan and The Order and The List. I told him of the risk of the Taras being called that night to die. Mike heard gibberish. He didn't understand.

Finally, I heard him agree. It was hard to hear him and Joseph over the reeling in my brain and the demands spewing from my own mouth.

I was afraid Mike was humoring me. I was afraid he didn't believe me at all. As a prophet of Christ, I had to make him understand.

I dismissed Mike and let him go back to sleep. He wasn't hearing or understanding me, so I tried to find another way to make him understand that the children had to start anew. I had to be sure everyone was on board with The Plan. I had to be sure the world would be rebuilt. I had to be sure it was okay to die. I was scared. I sent out more messages on Facebook. I tried to explain to Mike. He was tired. He was confused. He had to work in the morning. He had no idea what was happening. I had a very clear understanding that I was dying, but it was okay. I knew I had to remain calm and accept my destiny for the greater good. The experience was so foreign that those who loved me could no longer recognize me. I couldn't recognize myself. I wondered why I was the chosen one.

Finally, I must have fallen asleep.

Rebirth

I woke up Monday morning in my bed: alive. I knew I selected death, so I was confused to wake up in the world I had just agreed to leave. I was ecstatic to realize I died and was reborn into eternity feeling very similar to the way I felt before dying. I wondered which Tara decided to live to save the earth, but that investigation had to wait. It was my birthday, and I was ready to reunite with all the believers. I died and was born new in Christ. I danced naked.

I ran downstairs. Mike and the kids were at the dining room table. I wasn't in what I thought a heaven should look like. I realized they were all saved by Jesus. I died the night before and was saved and surrounded by all that was good. Mike was relaxed and calm. He made breakfast for the children. I assumed he knew all along what had happened the night before and was waiting for me to join him as a bona fide Christian that morning. I thought that is why he wanted me to fall asleep; he knew I would have a glorious born-again start if I accepted Jesus' mission. I figured he had direct orders to not interfere with God's plan, because I needed to experience the torment to grow in my path as a Christian. I had to be alone in my decision to follow the Lord.

As I processed this new understanding of my world, I started calling for my mother-in-law, who the family calls Gran, thinking she was at the door.

"Gran!" I called as I danced, still undressed, to the back door.

She was not there. I knew she was visiting to welcome me to the good life, so I deducted that she was hiding.

I ran from front door to back, repeatedly.

"Gran, Gran, Gran," I called, unable to find her.

"Tara, she isn't here," Mike said about his mother who lived across the Great Lake in Michigan.

He looked frustrated and confused. He started to look the same sort of concerned that he had looked the night before. I didn't believe him; I thought he was tricking me. I continued to call for Gran, unsure why Mike wasn't celebrating.

I took a seat at the head of the oak farm table, which was handed down from my parents. Somehow, I was wearing my maroon terrycloth robe, but I didn't remember getting it, much less putting it on.

Was it possible that Mike didn't remember my passage with Jesus, I thought, as confusion set in. Mike was with me. However, he acted like it was just an ordinary day, not one to excitedly celebrate. He kept trying to calm me down.

"Just sit down, Tara," he said. "My mother is not coming. You have to relax."

"No, she is here! She told me she would come to my birthday party," I said. "Today is my birthday."

I got up from the table and searched for her again, thinking she was hiding someplace in our modest three-bedroom house. I searched the boys' bedrooms, not as frantically, but still determined. I knew she was there for my birthday, but I couldn't find her. Mike guided me back to the table and had me sit down. I slouched, defeated.

"Where is she?" I asked Mike.

"She's home in Michigan," he said.

"Call her," I begged. "She promised she would come to my party."

I knew what happened the night before, but it seemed like Mike forgot. I tried to explain it, to remind Mike.

"The plan," I said.
"The order."
"The list."
"My birthday."

"Shhh, be quiet, Tara," he said to me gently. "You're scaring the kids. You have to get dressed. Please, Tara, go get dressed."

The mission was accomplished. I did my part and arrived in Eternity. Mike was acting like he didn't understand. I needed to communicate in a way he would remember that I died for Jesus.

I couldn't sit at the foot of the table any longer. I had to move around to get the grease in my brain working. I swayed side to side. I hopped up and down. I paced back and forth as I muttered to myself. I searched the corners of my intellect to find a way to connect with Mike. I needed to have him celebrating.

I made up a rhyme of words to spark understanding. I used simple language strung together to remind him of what had happened. I sang. I danced. I spoke in rhymes trying to share the good news.

"I was lost
I paid the cost
But now am here
My Michael dear
I died last night
It wasn't such a fright
I was born anew
To share forever with you
I adhered to the plan
I really understand
Dance and sing with me
Share the glee
Let's celebrate

My entrance at the gate…"

I peripherally noticed the horror and fright on my children's faces and Mike trying to reign in some piece of sanity. I couldn't recognize his efforts to help me, because I was beginning to see that I was the only one who knew of Jesus' plan. At that point, I didn't feel crazy or insane. I felt frustrated. It was them I had to convince; I already knew what was true.

"Tara, you aren't making any sense," Mike said. "Please go upstairs and get dressed."

At that moment, I thought Mike was annoyed and I didn't want him to be. To please him, I went upstairs and found my finest coat. I put it on to cloak myself in modesty. I was wearing only my finest coat as I twirled back down the stairs. Mike thought I was trying to seduce him. He seemed to get angrier.

"What are you doing?" He asked, patience long gone from his voice.

"I'm ready for my birthday party," I told him.

"Just wait," he said, as he picked up his cell phone.

I was left alone with my thoughts and figured out Ellen DeGeneres must be involved in the plan, because she's a lady who knows how to have a good time. I regained my glee at the realization that Ellen was going to throw my birthday party. I thought she was coming to my door to surprise me. Again I ran through the house. This time shouting her name.

"ELLEN!?"

"ELLEN?!"

"Oh my GOD! Ellen! I love you."

"ELLEN?"

"Where are you hiding?"

I couldn't find Ellen in the house. I stopped and thought. Then it came to me; Ellen was at her studio with an audience full of guests. She had arranged a grand affair. She was part of

The Plan too. She would surprise me with a party. Okay, I thought, I would act surprised.

Mike was pacing now in the back of the house at the breakfast nook. I didn't see my children and had no idea where they were (looking back, Mike probably had them set up watching cartoons). I waited patiently for him to get off the phone. When he ended the call, I started to tell him about Ellen's party. But he shushed me when his phone rang again.

I thought it was Ellen herself calling him from her packed studio in LA. Her audience was filled with Christians who were in on the plan ready to celebrate my entrance to Eternity. She had me on speaker phone. I was unable to contain my excitement. Mike handed me the phone.

"ELLEN, Ellen is that you?"

Ellen wasn't on the phone. It was my friend, Catherine.

"Are you coming to my party?" I asked.

"Uh, what... Tara. Are you okay?" she said.

Pissed, I handed the phone back to Mike.

"I need you over here NOW," he said to the phone.

Was my surprise to come later? When would we leave to go see Ellen? I remained happy but so confused. Why was everyone tricking me?

My mother-in-law was still missing. I needed to see her. I searched the house for her again, calling her name when I remembered that she was hiding.

"Tara, my mother is NOT in the house," Mike told me. "What are you doing?"

I ran from door to door again. I expected to find Mike's mother.

Agitation and anger consumed me. I considered smashing the dishes. I didn't understand why I had to wait for my party. I didn't understand why what I knew was true was different from what was happening. I knew my mother-in-law came to see me, but I couldn't find her. I was frustrated that no one else seemed to know about my birthday party. I thought Mike was pulling a trick on me.

As I stewed, I again became happy when I realized that Mike was mad because I figured out his surprise for me. With a silent vow to myself to settle down and to act surprised, I again became comfortable in my faith and knowledge that it was the day the Lord had made and set aside for me. With this enlightenment, I had to humor Mike and play along.

Mike was on his phone again; presumably talking to his mother. I was sing-songing in the dialect of a Southern debutante. I told a lengthy story about how fine and divine life was. I impersonated a caricature of a Southern belle.

"Tara. Shhhh," he interrupted me. "You have to get dressed."

As I dressed upstairs, I surmised my party would be a grand affair and everyone would come dressed in their party best. The scope of Mike's surprise to welcome me to genuine Christianity included a makeover. He ordered a dress and that was waiting for me on the shores of Lake Michigan. Oh, of course, I thought. The beach was the most beautiful place in the world, and Mike loved the water. He arranged for all my friends to be there, and of course, Ellen would be at the lake and dance with me. I thought then the phone calls Mike made were to square up details. Happiness returned at the thought of being surrounded by believers and wearing a beautiful, flattering dress, which Mike had picked out just for me. It was waiting at the lake in a makeshift model's studio. This was to be the best surprise Mike could have ever set up for me.

In that moment, I continued to rationalize. He was part of The Plan. The realization that he actually was saved years before and was waiting for the day that I would arrive was comforting. He and his mother had cooked up this grand affair just waiting for my number to come up. They couldn't have known when my number would arrive, but they both had been through it, and just needed time to put the finishing touches on the preparations in order. My mother-in-law was traveling. Mike just called her that morning to tell her that I had finally arrived.

For the first time in a long time, I felt worthy of love. I felt genuinely good and pure. Heaven was here on earth. I never knew. I just arrived that morning, but in that moment I understood that Heaven is a place where the believers walk among those who are yet to be saved.

Since I would be getting a makeover, it didn't matter what I wore. I pulled on a pair of ratty jeans and a soft, gray shirt that ended at the widest part of my hips. I wrapped my finest coat around me, and I danced down those hardwood stairs once more ready for the party.

Catherine arrived at the door looking terrific. She wore a long dress and her blonde hair was free, resting past her shoulders. Her made-up face hid any flaws. I knew she was coming for my party. She had to wait with the kids, while I went ahead to the lake and got transformed into a fine beauty.

"I'm going to be beautiful just like you," I said. "Mike has a makeover waiting for me."

Again I spoke in the grand language of a Southern belle telling her the entire story of my passage with Jesus. I was excited to convey my knowledge with her.

"Shh, Tara. My God Tara," she said. "Shhh."

So I talked in a hushed voice and sang.

"Life is great. I have found all the finer things. I now know the secrets that the believers and people of the fine life have known all along. I believe. I really believe. I believe in Jesus Christ."

"Shhh, Tara," Catherine said.

"Finally, after all this time, I am one of you. I belong. I am a Christian. I overcame doubt, which had always trumped faith. Look, I knew this day was coming. I was preparing. I bought these Corelle dishes," I said. "Isn't this a miraculous invention, dishes that do not break."

I grabbed a small, white coffee cup and smashed it on the floor. I saw it bouncing up whole.

"These dishes are divine," I said, pleased to share my knowledge with her.

She said, "Oh Tara."

She looked down and I then noticed the shards of glass from a broken mug.

"The broom's in the kitchen next to the desk. We have to leave. NOW," Mike told her.

I sensed his urgency. Oh yes, I thought, it was time to go to my party.

Mike seemed panicked. His body was tense. I understood it was because there were a lot of details with pulling off a big party like the one in store for me.

"It's time to go now," he told me.

"I'll see you at my party," I told Catherine as I walked out the door.

"This is a nice ride," I told Mike as I slid into the leather seats of his Saab.

We were driving toward Lake Michigan. I was in a joyful, peaceful place. We stopped at a building that I never noticed in all my years living in the same town. It must have been built overnight, I reasoned. As we pull into the expansive parking lot, confusion returned.

"Why are we stopping here? Aren't you taking me to the lake?" I asked Mike.

"This is part of the plan," he said.

I believed him, relieved that he finally acknowledged the plan. I reasoned that he couldn't tell the kids, who had to be sheltered from the knowledge. They needed to keep their sense of wonder. I felt glorious and inhaled a deep breath of fresh air as I twirled my way to the door.

Inside, I saw a nurse, who at the time I was convinced was my old friend Missy. She asked lots of silly questions. I made funny faces at her. I was bored and anxious to get to my party. I had no idea where we were and wondered if I always had known how whimsical Missy was. Mike was telling a lady at a counter about my arrival and was squaring up details for my party.

A short time later, we were on our way again. But we were driving west away from the lake, and then drove north on Interstate 43 alongside the lake, not toward it.

Mike talked on and on, but I can't remember anything he said. It was calming and I relaxed into the ride, enjoying being together that sunny and warm day.

Hell and Back

I was in a world where time didn't exist. I was trapped in Hell or maybe purgatory, I thought. Jesus came and went. I didn't know if I was dreaming or if I really was residing in the underside of the afterlife. With certainty, I understood I had died.

Not this again, I thought as I was returned to a bed. Visions came to me after they put me in that bed. I longed to be awake and explore the halls of a place that resembled something between a hospital and a prison. I didn't know where I was, but I felt trapped between two worlds; neither of them was familiar and both of them were frightening. It was as if I was being tugged by a heavy rope over a mud puddle lurching back and forth, clinging to the twine afraid to fall. I looked for a way to escape the pain and confusion. In the bed, I woke with fresh images of Hell through the ages.

I crawled from my bed to a door and then turned on hands and knees as I made my way through hallways seeing people — really just their faces. They stared at me. I didn't know why. They didn't talk to me. They didn't have expressions. They sat on couches dressed in navy blue sheets hiding their bodies. Other people were dressed with white pants and colorful-patterned sheets; they gathered at the end of the hallway enclosed in a box.

I wanted to ask questions, but I lost my voice. I only had expressions. My face crumpled with pleas. I looked around for someone help me, explain where I was. The place was weird; I had never been anywhere like it. I believed I was dead. I believed I was in the afterlife. The only truth I knew was my journey with Jesus. I was afraid I didn't make it to heaven, afraid I somehow blew it. I pondered my transgressions, my judgments of people. Now I needed people to help me, forgive me.

The people in blue sheets stared at me, their faces stuck in place. They neither looked away nor at me.

The colorfully dressed ladies found me crawling on the linoleum floor. They picked me up. It took two of them. Each grabbed me under the armpit and tugged me upright. They made me walk, each flanking me to steady my heavy steps. They gave me a Dixie cup of water and put me back to the bed. They rolled me over and injected a needle in my ass. I fought this mentally, even though I just laid there having lost most motor skills.

I wanted to scream, "NO!" I wanted them to allow me to stay awake. They were methodical and gave me the shot anyway. As a result, my eyelids grew heavy and involuntarily closed.

I returned to the world trapped with visions, which were the opposite of the grand voyage I had of arriving in a world of believers. I feared I was denied Heaven. I feared God determined me unworthy. Helplessly, I squeezed those lids tight trying to block out the vision.

I witnessed damaging pictures of a world wrought with disaster and humanity at its worst and most evil. I visited an unsophisticated Hell on Earth through the ages. I did not participate in these tragic incidents but hovered over them with Jesus as my guide, like Ebenezer Scrooge visiting the Christmases with the ghosts of past, present, and future: I couldn't interact with the cast of characters I witnessed.

Jesus waited to hear when I had seen enough. He wanted my approval to leave Him behind and go back to my life. One scene referenced the slaughter of the Jews. Then, I saw desperate Jewish parents starving their children in the hopes that the children would become small enough to be accepted into a non-Jewish family and given a chance to avoid the concentration camps and death sentences surely to come at the hands of the Nazis. Being of German descent, I assumed responsibility for this tragedy, despite having no evidence that my direct ancestors were Nazis. I knew my paternal grandfather actually fought on America's side in WWII as a seaman in the Navy, but I still felt responsible for Hitler's slaughter because of my more ancient German heritage.

"My people did this," I said. "My people who lived as farmers on the Messiah River in Germany were part of the Hitler movement. They bred the German soldiers who would carry out the horrific tragedy. I am so sorry. My soul is tainted from the bloodshed by the Germans. I am German. Forgive me, Jesus."

This nightmarish journey depicted fictional images stored in my subconscious bank of horror. I saw women raped at the hands of their husbands. I saw other women so severely tormented and tortured in incidents of domestic violence and mind control. I saw the prostitution of women. I felt sick at my flippant attitude toward feminists, previously unaware they were fighting to protect my generation from these injustices toward women. Those images planted an understanding of my mother and the grandmothers before her and their efforts that gave my gender a voice. I had thought women just wanted the right to work and vote; I forgot about their dignity. Women were fighting for freedom and choices and opportunity.

"I vow to join the sisterhood of woman to protect the rights gained by previous generations," I told Jesus. "Please forgive me for disrespecting my mother and her liberal views. Please give me another chance. I will fight for equal pay and equal rights. I will work to bridge the still-present gap between men and woman. I am responsible for the treatment disparity between men and women. I am so sorry."

Jesus said nothing in return; He guided me to the next image.

I saw poverty in families across the world. I realized my childhood financial struggles were not real poverty. I forgave my parents. I let go of the resentment at their decisions and circumstances that held us from being rich.

I told Jesus, "I will respect the working class. I understand what my father had always believed when he told me about America being the greatest country on earth. I respect his honor of service as laborer. I understand this country was built on the backs of workers like my father. These generations gave me opportunity and the chance to believe in the American dream. I will not squander this chance."

"I will have pride in where I come from. I will celebrate the sacrifices made by the military to protect my freedoms. I will feel blessed with the option to earn a living. I will respect the government systems that give to those families needing access to basic human rights," I told Jesus. "Please forgive me for my jealous attitude toward the rich and my bitterness toward the working class and my disgust of the dependent. Forgive me for believing circumstance was a choice. Forgive me for misunderstanding that my 'poor' childhood in this country was really rich in comparison to those living in third world countries and to the severely poor in this country. Please forgive me for not appreciating all the love You gave me."

Jesus told me how good my life was in comparison to the human suffering I witnessed. Many evils were personified and displayed before me, and I couldn't find a way to make them stop. I just wanted them to stop so I could go home to my family. I now regretted my decision to die. I thought I was trapped in Hell. I thought I made the wrong decision to die too soon, that I should have stayed alive long enough to right my wrongs.

Jesus left me, thus stopping the journey. I woke again in the strange room. I wondered if I needed to navigate through this place to reverse my decision to die.

Again, I crawled from my bed, heading out a door and down a hallway. I looked for an escape. I found a heavy door, which enclosed what I perceived to be a station. I tried the handle, but was stopped by a person with a colorful blouse carrying a cup of water; she guided me back to the bed I had just escaped. I begged her to let me up, but my language was just noises erupting, frantic and incoherent. I begged her to let me free from the nightmares. I wrestled. I pled. I was held down against my will. I was jabbed in my ass with another dose. This dose brought again the visions of Hell and human suffering.

Sometime later, the nightmare ended and I again woke in the darkened room. It may have been night or day; I had no way of knowing. I sought an escape creeping through halls heavy with excessive doses of forced sleep, but I could not walk. I saw a woman who looked like someone I knew, someone who was a domestic abuse survivor was clearly alive and in front of me. I couldn't place her name. Theresa? Wendy? I sat by her on a hard couch. I slouched into myself, trying to hide from the ladies with their needles.

"Cindy?" I asked, hoping she was someone I knew.

She shook her head, not knowing me.

"I am so sorry," I tried to say and repeat; it came out as mumbling.

She smiled at me. I petted her hand, because it was difficult to talk. She didn't move away. She was kind and compassionate. I didn't deserve it but was sincerely grateful for it. She was not evil. There were good people in the hallways. I needed to be with them. I waited on the couch for the Dixie cup of water that was sure to come; I noticed the colorful ladies spotted me despite my efforts to hide, to blend in with those people who were free from their beds.

The woman beside me leaned close and whispered, "Try the juice. Cranberry juice helps."

Hoping she was right, I tried to ask a lady with a shirt patterned with Easter eggs for some juice.

"Juice," I stammered, unable to really talk.

"Do you want some juice?" the plump lady replied.

Exhausted from the efforts of speech, I could only nod and hope she understood.

She complied. It was the sweetest juice I ever drank.

"More," I said desperately as I made sign language for the word "more" with my hands cupped and fingers tapping back and forth in front of my face like I had taught my children to do in their infancy.

"More," I repeated out loud in a strained voice.

"Do you want some more juice?" she asked.

Again I nodded. I wanted to keep drinking the juice. I followed her to the "station" where the juice was held. I held my hands open awaiting the blood of life. I wanted to drink as much juice as possible, but I was denied another serving.

Instead, I was ushered back to my room where another dose of medication was injected. I struggled, thrashed, tried to ask her to not give me any more shots. I couldn't communicate. I couldn't say a word, but my motor skills were returning. I could toss and turn. I could thrash and reach my arms behind me to guard against the invasion. However, these attempts were fruitless. I felt violated, abused, and helpless as they carried out this procedure over me. I was forced to travel to Hell again. I wanted to stop that loop, but I didn't know how.

The Unit

Wearing navy blue hospital scrubs, I sat sideways on a bed. I saw rumpled covers around me as I faced another bed, which had tightly-wrapped corners. I looked past the bed and noticed a locked window. A woman, who looked like my aunt Tina, came into the darkened room and stood over me. She handed me a pill and a Dixie cup of water as she reached for the light above my bed.

"Are you Tina?" I asked her.

"No," she answered and told me her name, which I didn't store to memory.

I didn't believe her completely. The resemblance of this woman to my aunt Tina was striking. Both women had that polished look of a clear complexion achieved with skillfully-applied makeup covering any flaws. I choose to believe this woman was my aunt dressed in a nurse's costume. This situation was foreign; I needed to find a way for it to make sense. I was anxious to try to understand where I was.

"Your hair?" I said. "I like your hair. It's pretty."

I lost my vocabulary somehow, and I couldn't find the right words to express my question. Trying to be nice, she replied that I was pretty too.

I shook my head and said, "Well, yes, thank you. But you. Your hair. It's dyed. It's styled," I struggled to go on. "You didn't get that done here. Where did you go? Can I go, too?"

She seemed amused at my complete lack of understanding. I didn't know where I was, but I needed to go home. I needed to find a way to where my life waited. I remembered a visit to bliss and a journey through Hell, but I couldn't reconcile these as real or fake. Maybe they were both. I didn't know where I was. At the time, I had no idea that I was recovering from a psychotic break. I recognized the place as a hospital, but I was not convinced it was real. It could have been built the day I arrived, because my son and his friends rebuilt the world Palm Sunday night, I thought then.

I thought about Easter Sunday, but I couldn't figure out if I missed the day. I didn't know what day it was or how long I'd been at the facility. I wanted to be home for Easter. I was afraid I might have to spend the rest of my days there in that place of oddity where time disappeared and wakefulness was limited, because I kept waking up in the same bed in the same room. I started to wonder if I lived there.

A nurse appeared in my room again. She was a stranger to me, different from the nurse who looked like my aunt Tina.

"What day is it?" I asked. "How do I get home for Easter?"

She answered simply, "Eat your food and take your medication. You have to stop fighting with us."

I didn't remember fighting with her or the other women dressed as nurses. She walked out of my room, leaving me alone to wonder where the food was and what medicine I was supposed to take. I was not hungry or sick, so her advice only added to my confusion.

I paced and surveyed my surroundings. I found a private bath and stepped inside. I took off my elastic-banded pants with stiff, navy blue fabric and the matching, boxy top and left them in a heap in the corner. I turned on the water, tested it with my hand, and stepped inside the shower partition. I drew the cheap, plastic, ivory-colored curtain closed. I noticed some sample-sized soap and shampoo. Maybe I am at a hotel, I thought, finding that idea comforting. I stood beneath the hot water and cleansed myself. I couldn't wash the confusion away, but I managed to remove a layer of gunk that had cloistered me from society.

Afterward, I toweled off and walked naked through the room to the cabinet where I had seen a brown, paper grocery bag of my clothes earlier. I pulled out a pair of underwear but decided to skip the bra. I dressed in jeans, a long-sleeved ivory turtleneck, and a short-sleeve, soft, grey shirt over that. I put on my ballet flats and made my way back to the bathroom.

I found a white, institution-issue toothbrush with standard, even bristles. The bristles were hard and didn't maneuver around the curvatures of my teeth well — it was cheaply made and brandless. I found another brandless item: roll-on antiperspirant. I was puzzled, so I removed the cap, touched the ball with my index finger and rolled it. The solution coated the ball. I saw my quizzical face in the mirror, raised a questioning eyebrow, and then shrugged my shoulders at my reflection. I lifted my arm over my head and reached under my shirts to apply the antiperspirant to my armpit and repeated the exercise for the other side. I placed everything back as I had found it. I felt a bit like a guest and didn't want to disrupt the order and tidiness of the bathroom.

Then I turned and noticed the heap of hospital clothes. I swept them up and looked around. I wondered what to do with them. I found a tiny garbage can. I tossed the uniform inside. Then, I went to find something to eat.

I asked a nurse for directions. She sat me at a table in a small room where I was served an oversized beef burrito. In silence and alone, I unrolled the flour tortilla and used my hands to slide the grease-laden ground meat into the shape of a cross. I made a form of Jesus on the cross with some lettuce and sprinkled it with salsa to represent His blood. I prayed for a while, apologizing for my sins and begging to go home.

Then I noticed some beans and rice on the tray. I wanted to eat them, but my plate contained my masterpiece, and I couldn't eat them from their serving dishes, I reasoned. I was not uncivilized. I wanted to spoon a reasonable portion onto a plate.

"Can I have another plate?" I asked a lady who had come to check on me.

"You have one," she said, and she rolled her eyes and shook her head.

I felt I was making art, but finally resolved to scrap my masterpiece. I cleared my plate, stuffing my tortilla and its contents into an empty, plastic coffee cup. I must have drunk the coffee while making my crucifix. I used my napkin to clean my plate. I asked for more napkins, which a reluctant nurse brought me, but I couldn't get the grease streaks off the plate. So I flipped it over, pleased with my resourcefulness. I scooped portions of beans and rice from their dishes onto the upside-down plate. I ate a few bites.

Then I abandoned my food; I walked to a cupboard on the other side of the room and opened the door to find puzzles and games on its shelves. A heavy-set black woman walked in.

"Tamara? Are you Tamara?" I asked, because she looked just like my friend Tamara and I was searching for some recognition of the world I left behind when I died for Jesus.

This woman, who looked un-showered and lost, was wearing the same heavy, navy blue clothes I had on earlier.

"I'm Maggie," she told me.

Everyone in the ward seemed to have been sent by Jesus to represent someone from my life. I wondered why these look-alikes were planted there. What was Jesus trying to tell me?

I wondered if these were people I had somehow wronged. People I was supposed to see as Christians and treat with love.

I selected a puzzle from the cupboard and made my way back to the table, ignoring my plate of barely-touched food. I pieced the puzzle together quickly and stood back to admire a picture of earth taken from a satellite; the image was a snapshot of life from the abyss. The patient I knew as Tamara was looking at me in amazement.

"Wow, you are really good at puzzles," she said.

"I like puzzles," I said, almost apologetically, embarrassed by my showy talent.

Using a crayon, she jotted down a poem and gave it to me. The poem read:

> *I once met a girl Tara was her name*
> *She was awesome at puzzles and Yatzee was her game*
> *So fair and kind with a beautiful smile*
> *Such happiness in her eyes that shined with style*
> *Everyone can see her heart full of love*
> *May you always be blessed from the light up above.*

I read it and cried. This preschool-like poetry was another sign from Jesus, assuring me I was on the right path. I exchanged a knowing glance with the child-like woman and thanked her for my gift.

It was signed by a woman named Maggie Stick. That was my world at that moment. Rare moments of intermittent clarity where I was functioning and seeing people who saw me as whole were all I had to hold. I felt I was a lost child of God. I needed those friends or resemblances of friendships to guide me home.

Writer

I walked around the unit carrying a composition notebook wrapped in a leather sleeve. I didn't know where it came from; it was too nice to be part of the standard issue from the institution. I considered myself a writer, which was crazier than meeting Jesus in my mind. I carried this notebook with its blank pages and wondered what I was to write. Its pristine pages were too pure to scribble my incoherent thoughts. It was a prop I carried in this institution of mystery. I walked around telling anyone I met I was writer. It surprised me that this confession did not invoke the same sure-you-are responses that I received when I told people that I had met Jesus.

The staff wore nametags with their pictures and their first names stamped in large print, with their positions written in a smaller font. A young girl with blond hair and a fit figure looked to be in her early 20s. Her nametag said Elizabeth. I thought so much time had passed that she was my cousin's 7-year-old daughter "Lizzie" all grown up. I wondered how so much time had passed.

"Lizzie, is that you?" I asked.

The girl with the tag stamped "Elizabeth" nodded.

"I came to talk with you," she said.

I was amazed that she was all grown up. I was excited to see her grown and beautiful working in this half-way place, which I was coming to accept as a sanctuary where Christians recovered from crossing over to the good life. I read the letters "O" and "T" on her badge. My cognitive function would come and go; I was grateful for those times I could think and reason. I willed them to stay. I asked questions when I could, hoping to understand what was happening.

"Are you an occupational therapist?" I asked her.

She nodded.

"Do you want to talk?" she asked.

"Oh, I don't need to talk to you. I already know what I am. I am a writer," I said, hugging my notebook to my chest.

She walked away smiling, maybe laughing. I smiled too.

I sat on the corner of a stiff couch and opened the book. I slid my hand across the blank pages and considered what to write in the space. I explored the book and found the pen holder empty; then a nurse gave me a pen. I looked in the folder pockets at the front and back of the book. I saw the poem from Maggie on one side. I pulled it out to re-read it. I found a little yellow pamphlet with the title "Sobriety Creed." I paged through it but couldn't read the smaller fonts. Focusing my eyes for too long hurt my head. In fact, my brain felt physical pain when I tried to read.

I didn't know why the pamphlet was there — I was not an alcoholic or drug user. I scribbled the word "confused" on a blank page of the pamphlet-sized yellow book. I remained too intimidated by my fancy notebook to write in its pages.

There was some mistake. I knew I was not an alcoholic or drug user. Why was this pamphlet in my sleeve's pocket? Maybe the staff thought I was a druggie. I had to find a way to make them understand I was one of the Christians. No one believed me when I told them I met Jesus. No one believed me, yet they let me believe I was a writer. I looked around and saw others in the unit. They were not holding sobriety pamphlets. They were not holding anything.

I began to wonder if where I was trapped was a place shared with addicts, to disguise the work of the Christians

who were treating me as I recovered from my passage with
Jesus Christ.

Trapped

As I recognized with some certainty that I unwillingly was secured at the hospital, I looked for a way to leave. The pull to find a way out of the institution was like solving a riddle. I wanted to go home, which required maneuvering around the gatekeepers and their procedures. I wanted to prove to myself I could find the exit. It was the rabbit hole where I had fallen and everything was bizarre like in that Lewis Carroll adventure-land tale. In this place, I found myself awakening to a new life. It wasn't that I was just born, I was starting to realize. It was as if a new way of life was unfolded before me. I just had to trust the uncharted territory and my navigation abilities. I was lost spiritually, physically, completely. I was trapped in a place I could not leave without permission.

The facility was a somewhat like a haven after the frightening experience of losing it. I thought I had been soaring in a spiritual way. I interpreted the events of the plan and its aftermath as accepting that I had physically died and left behind my family. It was a miracle I was able to be reborn, and I hoped I could reconnect with my family and gain their forgiveness and acceptance and understanding.

The institution was my second chance at mortal life; I entered into a covenant with Jesus to live as a Christian. I had to find a way back to the life I left to make good all the hurt I had caused in the past. I had to make right the wrongs, like an addict in a multiple-step program. I had to find a way out, because God just planted me in a safe place to gain strength until I could walk on my own and carry out His work. It was an all-consuming conviction that I was a child of God, and I needed to find a way out into the world to do His work.

At the facility, people walked alone. Each of us was on a separate journey. I looked for something familiar to the outside world; I found magazines. Having lost the ability to really read, I saw only pictures. I began to rip the pages apart, carefully preserving images of items to scrapbook. I came across a gold star and ripped quietly around its form, afraid the nurses would hear me and scold me for ruining the magazine. The image reminded me of my son Joseph, who I saw as a star. I continued finding images to tear from the glossy pages for a while: a patch of daisies, a clear complexion of a young woman.

Then my husband and Joseph walked into the room. I lost my calm and began with gibberish. I wanted to tell them where I'd been and where I was. I wanted to tell them I wished to leave and return home with them. My ability to speak betrayed me. It was sporadic, disjointed like that of a stroke victim. I couldn't speak in sentences.

"Joseph. Sweet. Joseph. See. Me."

"Mike. You. Me. Easter."

They seemed to know where I was. They seemed unhappy. Their faces were painted with pity and helplessness. Naturally, they didn't understand me. There was an intangible distance between us, especially with 11-year-old Joseph, which was probably fear. I wanted to explain to them I was on a spiritual quest working to find my way home. They offered no advice on how I could leave, because I couldn't articulate my question. Instead they reassured me that I would be okay when they left me again there. They hugged me, not tight embraces, but rather awkward patting like you would exchange with a smelly great aunt. They told me they loved me and looked away.

"We want you to get better," Mike said. "Once you are better, you can come home. I have everything under control. We are all praying that you get better."

"Where?" I asked holding up my leather sleeve and notebook.

"I brought it for you yesterday," he said.

My face scrunched. Again I was lost and confused; I didn't remember having seen him since the day of my birthday party. Mike continued to talk, trying to help me understand.

"You were sleeping," he said. "I left it on your nightstand so you could write. Then a nurse told me being in your room was a violation, and I had to leave you."

Mike and Joseph left me then, alone in the quarters in so-called safe hands. I was left wondering if wellness was possible and how I might accomplish it. I was broken. I was lonely. I wanted to be with my family. I wondered if they were living normally like before the world ended for me. The riddle of leaving involved improving my health, but I didn't feel sick. I just felt confused. So. Damn. Confused.

I didn't understand why I was left alone without my family. I made my promise to Jesus, so why didn't I return to my life? I continued to struggle to communicate. I paced. I saw a window and looked outside. There was a wooden playground completely surrounded by barriers. The building I was standing in barred it on one side and another brick building stood across the playground on the other. It was a safe, hidden playground, with fences on both sides connecting the buildings. I couldn't see an access gate. The playground was also empty. I wanted to go to it. I wanted to play outside at the secret playground, which had been abandoned and forgotten, much like I was. I was sequestered from everything.

110

I wanted Mike. I thought my husband was a character from a Dr. Seuss book. I roamed the halls and quoted *One Fish, Two Fish, Red Fish, Blue Fish*.

"We like our bike. It is made for three. Our Mike sits up in back, you see. We like our Mike, and this is why: Mike does all the work when the hills get high."

I became more and more frantic, and I repeatedly asked for my Mike.

"Where is my Mike?" I asked no one in particular as I paced up and down the hallway.

"Mike does all the work when the hills get high," I told a different woman dressed as a nurse who had to try to calm me.

"Check out back," I said. "Mike is out back with the Yak. We have a Yak; he's out back."

"Find my Mike; he can do all the work because the hills are high," I said.

My song pleading for Mike was ignored. So I paced some more. Pacing relaxed me somewhat.

I walked around and found another window, this one was an interior window with criss-crossed etching. It looked into an enclosed room where nurses conversed with one another, desks sat piled with paperwork, and phones rested quietly on the walls. Across the rectangular nurses' station was another room similar to where I was, only all the people there wore regular clothes. The people there seemed awake. They looked as if they had somewhere to go. However, I was stuck with people mostly still dressed in hospital blues and wandering through the halls, or curling up in the fetal position on the couches, or sitting motionless on waiting-room chairs.

In the other room, I saw a man. He noticed me surveying the room where he stood. He looked lucid. I wanted to ask him questions. I didn't know how to get to him. I asked questions with my face through the glass separating us. He shrugged and waved me over.

"How do I get there?" I asked a nurse who just stepped through the heavy door that locked behind her.

"Wait," she said.

Without any other options and mentally exhausted and frustrated, I walked to my room. All the windows and doors facing out were secured. It began to seem that I was in a psych ward, though I had never been in one before. Everyone treated me like a child. I thought there was some mistake, because I was without my freedom. I was not crazy. I was not seeking to do harm, to myself or anyone else. I just wanted to find something familiar, tangible, or real. The place seemed phony with its odd rules and limited access to information. No one communicated with me what this place was called. I took a nap.

I woke up and walked to the door in my room. I didn't know what day or time it was, but I was still wearing my jeans and gray shirt. Though, right after waking, I felt less agitated and realized I had my wits about me. I turned left down a corridor after noticing a heavy metal door at the end of the hallway leading right. I found the windows to the other side again.

"How do I get there?" I asked a nurse, as I pointed through the windows to the place with people who looked closer to normal.

"Wait for the doctor," she said.

Soon, a middle-aged woman appearing confident and relaxed invited me to sit at a table in the room where I had eaten rice and beans and put together a puzzle. This woman, maybe the doctor, was wearing a smart pantsuit. She seemed to know me, but I didn't know her.

She asked me questions I didn't understand with a folder and a pen in her hand, then, she left me. I walked to my room and sat on my bed hiding my face in my hands. I slouched and saw my feet pointed toward the vacant bed across from me with its sheets and spread neatly tucked at the corners.

A nurse came into my room.

"You can go to the other side," she said.

The nurse picked up my paper bag of belongings and escorted me through the nurse's station to the larger room. We walked down a hallway, and I was really pissed to find a room just like the one I left. I was just as far away from home in these new quarters. I put my paper bag into the closet. I knew it was called a closet now. The day that I had showered, I couldn't figure out what it was called. My vocabulary, once lost, was returning.

The Other Side

I walked out to the common area of this similar, but new to me, wing of the hospital. It was bigger than the unit on the other side of the nurses' station. There was a TV on. I wondered if there was a television on the other side. I sat on a chair by the wall. In the new room, the chairs were situated around the perimeter of the large room, as if to discourage an intimate setting for the patients. There were only two people seated, each alone. An empty table was set up in the corner of the room on a linoleum pad. Vending machines offered snacks and soda. I presumed people could use money and make purchases from them, but my pockets were empty. As I began to orientate myself to my new surroundings, I did so without a guide. Jesus hadn't made an appearance since walking me through Hell. I was left with only His image. I was alone, and searched for clues and people I could trust to help me find a way back to my life.

I watched the people, but I didn't recognize anyone. On the other side were people who seemed like my friends; everyone I met there reminded me of a person who I knew outside the ward. Those people were planted to represent people I was supposed to forgive or understand better.

I sat on the chair with my sobriety notebook and writing tablet in my lap. Then I stood and turned to look through the windows of the nurses' station toward the unit of the facility I had left. I saw people in catatonic states. I saw blank stares on faces. I saw un-showered blobs lost, like I had been. I was still lost, but I sensed I was making progress. I turned and sat back down, sighing to myself and hugging my notebook to my chest.

The man I saw through the window when I was trapped on the other side came over and sat next to me.

"Where are we?" I asked him.

He had a mischievous grin, black hair, and a boney face. He was tall and dressed in faded jeans and a T-shirt.

"I am leaving today," he said.

I must have looked surprised to discover a person could leave.

He gestured to the left. I followed his gaze and noticed an unencumbered set of double-glass doors leading outside to a walkway. A parking lot was visible beyond the path.

I wondered again what day it was and whether or not I missed Easter. I hoped Mike would return and take me home. Time was impossible to track; I couldn't say for sure when my husband was last here visiting, but it seemed recent.

I left the man to collect more clues to the mystery of leaving this place. I walked down the hallway and found a room with a cabinet and a circle of chairs with nothing in the middle — no table, no TV, no rug — just emptiness. I opened the cabinet, which contained more games and puzzles, as well as craft supplies. I vaguely remembered the concept of art therapy and rolled my eyes: Playing with construction paper and crayons wasn't going to help me understand this foreign place. As I turned to leave the room, I noticed a sign on the door the times for group meetings such as alcohol and narcotic abusers. I had no concept of time, so I didn't know if these meetings had taken place or if they were for later in the day.

I went back to find the strange man, but he was gone. I wished I had asked the kind man more questions. I wished I would have asked him his name. I also wished I had asked why he was there and where I was, because I recognized he was more lucid than I was.

I didn't believe completely I was in a hospital receiving mental help, but I started to realize everyone else did. I held on to some confusion in order find a way to function within the world. I felt saved and also believed that I had to walk amidst the nonbelievers and disguise my knowledge of Jesus.

I considered the kind man a nonbeliever. I had looked at him and then looked at my notebook and its sobriety creed and thought he must be one of the alcoholics and not a believer. I thought the hospital was a place for those who crossed over to Christianity to recover from the experience, and it had to be shared with alcoholics and drug users to protect the public from realizing the real work of Jesus that was being conducted within its walls. I believed all those people I met on the other side were bona fide born anew Christians on a journey similar to mine. They needed to face their own demons in their life and break through before returning back to reality as children saved by Jesus.

I held onto this notion of Jesus, so I ignored that I was insane.

Escape

Mike and Mom came to visit me; they seemed happy to find me on this side of the window, which was measurable progress from the sequestered quarters of the other side. I was closer to the outside door – closer to the woman they knew. I recognized some pieces of reality, however distorted. I could walk around and talk in sentences.

"How are you feeling?" Mom asked.

"Is it Easter?" I asked in return.

"No, it's Friday," Mike said.

"Good Friday?" I asked.

They both nodded. I didn't ask what year it was, but it seemed years had passed. I began to wonder if my lengthy travels with Jesus happened while the world stayed still. I mulled over the possibility. I nodded hesitantly.

"Can I go home for Easter?" I asked.

"The doctor is coming. You have to eat," mom told me.

A cafeteria tray was placed before me as I sat in the large room with Mike and Mom seated at the table with me. They didn't have food set in front of them. I wanted to eat the meal but felt no hunger. I was confused as to what this eating was supposed to do for me. Nourishment wasn't something I was missing; it was information I hungered for. I wondered if they really knew what had happened to me, or if Jesus decided to keep them in the dark. Did I just have to keep the experience a secret?

I wanted to be home for the celebration of Christ's rising from the dead. I wanted to celebrate the rebirth of Christ as our Savior. I believed He died for my sins, and that I had been washed clean with my experience. I wanted to reconnect with Jesus with a Catholic Church Mass. The memories of little girls with hats and the floral patterns on the dresses of women in the pews was a picture I longed to see. I wanted to wear my own white sandals and receive the body and blood of Christ. I wanted to collect a small jar of holy water and shout "Hallelujah!"

My memory of the ceremony of the holy water being reintroduced in the church was beautiful. The priest walked down the center aisle and shook an object, shaped like a rattle with tiny holes, over the heads of the believers on either side of the aisle. As the drops of renewing water landed on the believers, they made the sign of the cross across their face and chest to represent the Father, Son, and Holy Spirit. This sign of the cross was a confirmation of their belief. Rejoicing music was sung among the faithful, and the general mood of the congregation was joyful.

I wanted to feel this joy and peace and be surrounded with its comfort and hope. Easter had long been my favorite holiday, and the promise of an early morning Mass motivated me to "get well" in the eyes of those gatekeepers who held me in that place of medicine and procedure.

My family and the professionals I encountered didn't believe any of my experience of meeting Jesus. Confusion plagued me. I never truly knew the definition of confusion before this experience. The confusion wasn't like when I tried to put together a puzzle or grasp complex organic chemistry in college. That confusion when I tried to figure out what day it was and where I was happened on an exponential level beyond puzzlement.

So, I decided to play along with their interpretation of the events.

"You had a nervous breakdown," Mom told me.

Mike nodded.

"You are at a psychiatric care center in Green Bay. This is a mental health hospital," he added. "You were in the intensive care unit yesterday. Do you know when you were moved to this unit?"

My head spun. I gasped. He sounded convinced and convincing. Yet it didn't match what I felt.

"If you listen to the doctors, they will let you go home," Mom said, offering me some advice I could follow.

I felt fine, not crazy. I didn't know what the doctors were instructing me to do or needing to hear from me. I needed to find a way to get my family, and especially Mike, to understand I was saved and, from this time forward, was committed to Christianity. I had to make them understand and reassure them it was okay; I was okay. I remembered the poem that Maggie wrote for me in the other unit. She had penned a confirmation, " ... blessed from the light up above." Yet, the only way to make the doctors release me was to stay quiet about those events of meeting Jesus and keep the story of salvation to myself. I nodded to myself as I became armed with a plan to convince the gatekeepers to set me free.

As we sat at the table, a woman who introduced herself as the doctor came to assess me. I recognized she was a doctor, but again she wore regular clothes, not a white overcoat. She carried a thick folder of paperwork. I prepared to answer her questions appropriately so I could go home.

"Do you know where you are today?" she asked.

"A hospital?" I answered with a question.

She nodded.

"A mental hospital," I continued, swallowing hard.

She nodded again.

"Do you know what day it is?"

"Good Friday," I said confident.

119

"Do you know what year it is?"

I shook my head and looked down. I was afraid I failed the test. Yet, she continued.

"Do you know you experienced a series of events that weren't real?" the doctor asked.

"Yes," I said, though I just humored her.

She talked more. My brain began to hurt again. It was different than a headache, but I felt actual, painful throbbing and strain as though my brain was separating and spilling to the edges of my skull. I phased in and out of attention. I could not focus on what she was saying. I only heard the words "psychosis" and "hallucinations" amidst a muddle of other words. The phrase "an episode of psychosis" stopped my brain and I got lost trying to interpret its meaning.

I was scared, because the recognition of these words and their meanings were being used to describe me, a rather normal person. People who were sane did not experience an episode of psychosis or hallucinations, I thought. Then, I could only logically conclude I was insane.

"Do you remember taking any drugs?" she asked pulling me back to the present.

"No, I don't use drugs," I told her, once again confident.

I hoped she would let me go home and understand that I didn't need that yellow notebook and its sobriety creed.

"What about Focalin?" she asked.

Shit, I thought, they caught me! I had taken a few of Joseph's ADHD pills to keep me sharp on occasion. Is that why I was there? I wondered. Did they think I was a drug abuser?

"Do you remember taking them?" the doctor asked.

"I only take them once in a while, to keep me sharp," I said. "I took one or two this weekend."

"Do you know you are in a hospital?" she asked again, unfazed by my confession.

I nodded.

"Do you know you experienced an episode of psychosis?" she asked.

There was that word again. Was she trying to say I was psychotic? I was scared, and I chose my words carefully. I did not think I was psychotic. I knew I met Jesus Christ. I couldn't tell her that, though, or she'd keep me locked in the mental hospital.

So instead I said, "I was somewhere else."

This seemed to please her. She jotted some notes, and with reluctance in her voice, she said I could go home.

"Mike and your mom can bring you home now. We just need you to sign some of these papers," she said.

I signed papers I was unable to read.

After learning they thought I had been psychotic, I was surprised she released me from the place they called a hospital. I was scared too. Up until that moment, I didn't realize the assumptions the staff and my family were working under to get me back to reality. I didn't realize I was classified as "psychotic" and had been an inpatient at a psychiatric center. My brain had physical pain again. It felt like a headache similar to a hangover when my brain matter seemed to swell to the edges of the skull and created a painful pressure. I cursed myself for dipping into Joseph's pills and wondered if I did it to myself. Yet I still thought they were wrong. What they were saying couldn't be true: I really met Jesus. Yes, that was a much more likely conclusion at that time. I chose to believe I was chosen and that Jesus disguised His work as — what was that phrase the doctor used — an episode of psychosis.

Mike and Mom walked me back to my room to gather my paper bag of clothing. I realized then that Mike didn't have time to find a suitcase. That day we drove to my "birthday party" I had no way of knowing we were, in fact, not together as I had thought. In that moment, I began to see I was alone in what the world saw as nonsense. I was traveling the depths of what the world called insanity while Mike was driving, focused on the road, trying to find me and bring me home once again. Ironically, bringing me back meant dropping me off into the care of others.

He knew he was taking me to this psychiatric care center for admission to its Intensive Care Unit for treatment. I knew we were driving on a sunny day. I was content. I didn't realize I was alone. I didn't realize while my feet still touched the earth, my being betrayed me. My mind had tricked me into a fantasy land where I was the star child of Jesus chosen to be saved that day. That "psychosis" swallowed me whole, spit me out, and shook loose everything I thought I knew about myself.

So Mike had left in a hurry and scooped up whatever clean clothes he could find for me and threw them in a bag quickly. Now, Mike carried the paper bag for me as we left the hospital. We walked through the same doors that the strange, kind man I met had exited through earlier.

I walked along the path and then slid into the back seat of Mike's car. We drove home. Now that the solution to the riddle had been revealed, I was no longer excited to be going home and I was no longer certain I had met Jesus. Maybe I was crazy. Maybe I made myself this way. Maybe it was my fault.

I began to remember some of the other things the doctor had said at the table while we made the 40-mile drive home to our three-bedroom house in Manitowoc.

"You suffered what used to be considered a nervous breakdown. Today, the medical community considers this loss of self a 'psychotic break,' which more accurately describes the insanity."

"Have you ever been told you have bipolar disorder?"

The answer to that question was no. Never. I stared out the window and wondered if I did in fact have a serious mental illness — and if so, if that meant I would forever be disabled and crazy.

PART THREE: THE REPAIR

April – September 2010

Easter Sunday

It wasn't a holy experience. The holiday I anticipated as a glorious confirmation of God's love for me and Jesus' resurrection from the dead was anticlimactic and happened without my contribution. The boys found Easter baskets, store-bought and packaged with cellophane, without me hiding them. Mike stepped into my designated role; he did the best he could.

We didn't go to church either. Instead, my family got together for a buffet at an area restaurant, where the food was not spectacular. Then, we went to Uncle Tony and Aunt Carol's ranch house with its well-cared-for backyard.

Everything was fine as we gathered outside in the sunny weather exchanging pleasant stories. Everything, that is, but me. I was in a fog. I hovered over the guests, unable to engage. I overheard the chatter, but I couldn't reach out and partake in the conversations. Focusing on just getting through, I tried to hide. Peripherally, I noticed my husband was drinking beer. I didn't like it when he drank. Not that he did anything wrong, but on those occasions when he exceeded his limit, his face sunk into his neck and his speech slurred and he lost some balance. He grew slower in motions, but overall he wasn't a "bad" drunk. In fact, I didn't think he was a drunk at all. Nonetheless, his drinking bothered me. His libations loosened his grasp of control. He lost his grace the times the alcohol was too readily available.

I drank too, on occasion, but on Easter no one offered me a drink. I was too fragile, too medicated. My speech remained delayed. My synapses fired, their connections retarded in my brain. I couldn't see things clearly. I couldn't interact. I was a wallflower on the day I had so eagerly awaited.

Under those circumstances, I began to feel agitated. I wanted to leave, but the boys were having fun with the egg hunt and were comparing their baskets' bounty with that of my two nieces each a year younger than my boys. Their ages that Sunday were 4, 3, 2, and 1.

So, despite this normal, peaceful gathering backdrop, anger and entitlement filled me when the taxation of being present escalated beyond my control. Rage, which I had tried to keep buried, escalated through my blood and demanded a release. I was ready to go home. I was unreasonable in communicating this. I felt trapped, again. Everyone else seemed to be having fun, and I didn't understand how they could be relaxed when I was in such a distraught state. I had only been released from the hospital two days earlier.

Mike agreed to take me home.

"You can't drive," I retorted.

"I'm fine," he answered.

"You are not fine," I said.

"Yes, I am fine," he said.

"You think you are going to put your wife and three kids in a car with you after you have been drinking?" I screamed.

The irrational rage snapped on suddenly like a storm, and it was violent.

I shook with rage. My eyes glazed as I stood in the kitchen with my family, children included. I didn't care. For me, it was just Mike and I on another standoff. I blamed him for my breakdown. I thought he should have helped me. I thought he didn't love me.

"Tara, come here," Mike said to me, with a table separating us.

"I am not a fucking dog!" I yelled.

The rage erupted. I rationalized he had it coming for ignoring me and having a good time while I was so obviously not feeling comfortable at the party. I was pissed; I thought it was a time when he was supposed to be taking care of me. I couldn't accept that he probably only had two beers and I was overreacting. I felt righteous and therefore justified in punishing him and inflicting my rant.

This narcissistic attitude was not something new. I often only saw my own needs for comfort and help. As a general course, I didn't respect others or even try to genuinely understand them. Usually, though, I refrained from starting fights with loved ones in public.

My family — trying to get between Mike and me — offered to drive us across town.

"No. I can fucking drive," I said.

"Tara, you can't drive," a voice from the crowd came back.

"Well, he certainly fucking can't drive," I said.

My children were there. Carol ushered them back outside, trying to spare them this scene of domestic violence.

"Tara, let us take you guys home," my father said.

"You've been drinking too," I screamed.

I was mad — mad at the world, mad at the family who was relaxing.

"I can drive you," my sober sister said. She hadn't drunk in years, and her husband was also a teetotaler.

"I can fucking drive," I screamed. "Get the damn kids."

"Tara, Tara, Tara," I heard from various patronizing voices trying to sooth and reach me.

I felt as if my head were about to explode. I wanted to be home. I wanted to get the fuck out of there. I wanted to be free of the pain. I wanted safety from the world and from myself. I wanted it all to stop. I held Mike responsible, because I couldn't face the fact I was the one to blame. I lost my shit, again. I couldn't keep it together. Jesus wanted me to celebrate his resurrection; I let Him down. I missed Easter.

Someone drove us home while I festered in the back seat. When we arrived, I was put to bed. In bed, I came back from rage to a place of remorse. These episodes of rage always left me hating myself and with no choice but to apologize and hope for forgiveness and then vow to never do it again.

As I calmed down, I was able to see how the previous week of my hospitalization had taxed Mike. He had to work, juggle the children who were on a week-long spring break, and worry about me. The doctors couldn't tell him how long I'd be gone. They had no way of knowing when the medication would start to work and restore sanity, and they had no way of knowing if I could recover. Like treating a fever, it could spike and worsen or subside and vanish. I was lucky. My psychosis lasted just five days. However, I would later learn the mania, which had spiraled to psychosis, continued to seep into the days and weeks and months following my release from the hospital. I would discover that mania was not always the heightened sense of joy or series of compulsive shopping sprees that you usually hear about from the media. In my case, mania was destructive and frightening.

The pillbox

Each morning throughout our marriage — and honestly even before — Mike brought a cup of coffee to my bedside table and left me to slowly wake and drink the fresh brew from a powder blue, beveled coffee mug, which was stamped with the popular phrase "Life is Good!" But those weeks following the break, I wasn't trusted to wake myself or even be alone. I might have stayed in bed, trapped in my head, trying to figure out what the hell had happened. Ironically, now that I was home I wanted to vanish. I was ashamed of myself.

Feeling so heavy and groggy from the Benadryl that sedated me the night before, I needed help getting up. Mike swung my legs around the bed, planting my feet on the floor to support me. I leaned on him and allowed him to pull me to my bare feet and then lead me down the stairs without showering.

In the kitchen, he showed me the pillbox resting on the butcher block adjacent to the stove. I didn't know exactly what was inside the partitions of the clear plastic case.

"Swallow me," the pills seemed to taunt.

Yet, I couldn't take the whole row, tempting as it seemed. Not just then. I had to first empty the square farthest to the left and throughout the day move across at prescribed times. This first square was filled with some pills of different sizes and colors. It was as if I was living in a halfway house. Sadly, if not for the blessing of my husband, I feared I would have resided in one. I vowed to be nicer to him so he wouldn't abandon me, again, to the care of strangers.

I knew I was fortunate to have Mike's commitment to love and support me during this sickness, more so since neither of us knew if health would return. I wasn't well when I was discharged from the hospital, but I had enough family support to be allowed to continue treatment at home. I was closely monitored. For what, I was not sure.

A piece of masking tape was stuck on top of the left square of the pill case with the word "Breakfast" scribbled in my husband's penmanship. Other squares had other words: "lunch," "mid afternoon," "dinner," and "bed." I couldn't crack the straightforward code and figure out what times correlated to these events. I didn't know what time to eat, or when the mid-afternoon was. I didn't know what time to go to bed. Heck, I couldn't even tell time on a regular clock anymore, but I could read the digits on the microwave. It was 8:08.

"Eat some toast," Mike said to me, as he handed me a cup of coffee and a plate of bread. I trusted him and accepted the pills he placed in my palm. I didn't gag from them. I just swallowed. They didn't make me feel any noticeable difference.

"At ten, we go to see Dr. Burbach," Mike said.

I knew Dr. Burbach. I unloaded my problems, and he assured me I was okay. We had met about five years earlier, when the middle-aged, athletic, intellectual type diagnosed me with dysthemia, a chronic low-grade depression that caused one's view of the world to be tainted with omnipresent, worse-case-scenario thoughts. Since then, I had seen Dr. Burbach off and on when depression interfered with my day-to-day responsibilities. At those times, he told me I had double depression, when life events had pushed me into a debilitating case of hopelessness on top of the chronic blues.

During those episodes of major depression, I would contemplate suicide. Able to recognize these fatalistic thoughts as extreme scared me enough to seek treatment. My thoughts would include rudiment, constant reeling, images and sensations and plans. Some images were of me hanging dead from a belt in the shower. Others were a satisfying shattering of my brain with a bullet through the mouth, which would scatter my skull into smithereens. However, guns scared the shit out of me; I didn't own one then and never would. I thought about the cleaning that must be done to remove slivers of skull and blood from the carpets after a suicide. A police officer once told me that at a scene of a gunshot wound to the head there were shards of skull sliced into the walls, a detail I left out of my news article that appeared in the following day's newspaper. When I wasn't so dramatic, I made plans to overdose on drugs and researched effective elixirs on the internet. All these scenarios had the same climatic result: death at my own hands. However, I never actually attempted suicide.

I also wrote letters in my head to the loved ones I would leave behind. This always choked me up. I would get scared of those thoughts, but couldn't get them to stop on my own. They would come uninvited and persist. So, scared, I sought additional treatment from Dr. Burbach in the form of psychotherapy. He'd also refer me to a medical doctor who would prescribe Wellbutrin, an antidepressant that was easily accessible.

This little pill worked. In a matter of weeks, I bounced back to run-of-the-mill melancholy, which was a constant companion throughout my adult life. These chronic blues were a welcome respite from the major depression that visited and vanished, leaving me guilty of its destruction. Sometimes the destruction took the form of missed deadlines. Other times, it was lost friendships from rage or ignoring my side of the friendship relationship. While depressed, even the idea of taking a shower was too much to bear. And certainly, the thought of actually going into public was agonizing. Sometimes, when work was too big a struggle, I left the office headed to an "appointment," "meeting," or "interview" just to escape to my apartment and bury myself beneath a heavy comforter with the heat turned too high. I was irritable; especially annoyed by those people around me who seemed so fucking happy. I hated them.

I had accepted the idea that I would always be plagued with melancholy and that I could find some relief with medication. So I had taken antidepressants off and on for at least a decade. I usually stopped taking it once I felt "better" or when the hassle of running back to the medical doctor for refills and explaining my depression took too much gumption to muster.

None of that explained my most recent, so-called psychosis and new diagnosis of bipolar disorder. I was an invalid, whose self had been destroyed by insanity. Sanity, I believed, was a state within my control. I was irritated that I needed medical treatment to be able to handle life cheerfully. I didn't see the events that had occurred as necessarily medical, but rather weakness. I shook off these thoughts and took my coffee, in that mocking Life is Good mug, out to the front porch with a cigarette and a lighter. I sat on the cold cement stairs and smoked. A bicyclist wearing a T-shirt and wind pants rode past. A couple walked across the street pushing a stroller, as a baby about 10 months old waved chubby hands in delight. I inhaled deep, slow breaths. I exhaled quick bursts of pollution. I walked back inside. Thomas and Joseph had left for school without me helping them to do so. Alex was watching PBS morning cartoons lying on the area rug with a snuggle blanket.

"Are you coming with me to see Dr. Burbach?" I asked Mike.

"Yes. I'm driving," he said.

I knew I couldn't drive, even at low speeds. I was not allowed any independence in my disabled state.

"I mean, are you coming back to sit on the couch with me?" I asked, annoyed.

"I was planning to. Is ... is that okay?" he said, almost as if he had to tiptoe around me.

"Sure," I said. "What are we going to do with Alex?"

"Carol is coming," he said. "You should probably go take a shower."

Carol is my godmother and my aunt. I attended her wedding to my mother's brother in a green dress at the age of 4. I knew this from the Polaroid snapshot kept in an album at her house, not because I remember the wedding. But I do remember my baptism, which I received late at age 7. I also remember her staying with her on weekends and going to the library, the park, the beach or the zoo. Every time I made her beef stroganoff recipe, I remembered happy childhood memories.

Carol had taken care of my family since I'd been sick. It seemed everyone who cared for me wanted me to believe I was sick, not crazy. Since suffering what used to be considered a nervous breakdown (I couldn't really stomach the idea of calling it a psychotic break), they told me I shouldn't use the word "crazy."

"You are not crazy," they said. "You are just sick."

Ill, I thought, mentally ill. I was crazy, despite what they thought I was able to hear and understand. I was either crazy or I really met Jesus Christ. Neither idea offered much comfort.

Carol filled my cupboards with groceries, including things I never would have bought myself, like boxed mashed potatoes. Still, I was grateful the family had food. She left inspirational note cards around the house for me to find. And now that I was home, she watched the boys every time Mike took me to see a doctor.

Going to see Dr. Burbach was like going to a doctor and pulling down my pants. But rather than donning a gown and physically revealing myself to him, I sat on the corner of his couch and answered his questions. He poked and probed at the innermost thoughts tucked in my brain. Still fragile, I continued to get headaches. I felt a physical expansion and contraction of my spilled brain matter.

When Carol arrived, she was cheerful and well intentioned.

"How are you feeling?" she asked.

Still slow in my speech I said, "Okay."

Mike was in go-mode and I quickly was ushered to the car for my appointment. I slid onto the leather seats, warmed from the sun.

After a short drive to the lakefront office building, we were greeted by Jill at the desk. I took a green apple Jolly Rancher from the candy dish at the counter and sat in the waiting room. I recognized a NAMI (National Alliance for the Mentally Ill) brochure on the end table closest to me. I wondered if I needed help from that organization. I wondered if I was that far gone. But we weren't in the waiting room long before Dr. Burbach stepped in to greet us.

"How are you folks doing today?" he asked.

"Fine," we both said in unison.

We were fine, I guess; what other way was there to be? And even if the stress of Mike doing everything and me trapped in an invalid state was clearly not fine, we were both proud enough to fib a little bit. Dr. Burbach ushered us into his tiny room, took a seat, picked up a folder of paperwork, and gave us both the once over. We sat on either side of his grey couch, not close enough to touch — a comfortable distance separated us. Discomfort filled the room. We had to talk to ease the pain.

"How are you doing, Tara?" he asked.

"Fine, I guess," I said.

I left out the feelings of inadequacy, the confusion, the embarrassment, the helplessness of being incapacitated, and the degrading neediness as we navigated the post psychosis landscape.

Dr. Burbach looked at Mike, who nodded but didn't elaborate. Dr. Burbach then began to remind me I was there because I was recovering from a psychotic break — as if I could forget. The word again, it remained hard to hear. He told me I had a series of hallucinations and delusions.

"Can you tell me about them?"

I recounted my meeting Jesus for what felt like the 100th time. I tried to tell him the details of the death countdown, the birthday party, and traveling through Hell; but then, he swayed the conversation back to present day. He said there were no health benefits to be gained by looking backward.

"None of that happened," he said. "It is like someone who is on a drug-induced trip."

"They weren't hallucinations or delusions, like you say. They were real," I said. "It really happened."

I was getting agitated, but knew I had to reel that in. If I was too unstable, they may have returned me to the hospital. I trusted Dr. Burbach completely. He might have been the only one to help me. I held onto the tale of Jesus. Somehow it was easier to believe I met Jesus than to reconcile His visit as a hallucination and therefore a symptom of a mental illness, namely bipolar. I wanted to be special and chosen rather than helpless and crazy. I wanted there to be a value in the visions I experienced, which I eventually would come to accept as nonsense.

Dr. Burbach explained a hallucination as a sensory experience of something that does not exist outside the mind, caused by various physical and mental disorders, or by reaction to certain toxic substances, and usually manifesting as visual or auditory images. I liked how he didn't talk down to me, even if maybe he was, as if he understood that I had the intellectual capacity to follow his clinical explanations. The word hallucination originated between 1640 and 1650. It came from the Latin allūcinātiō, which means a wandering of the mind. This mind wandering idea sounded poetic.

"Think of it like a drug-induced experience," he told me again.

"I wasn't hallucinating. I know what hallucinating is," I said. "I don't use drugs, I never took LSD. Maybe I just had delusions."

Delusion seemed a word of less severity. In psychiatry, it means a fixed false belief that is resistant to reason or confrontation with actual fact.

Dr. Burbach told me spiritual undertones or connotations were common in hallucinations. Common: now there's a word I didn't think I'd come across in a description of my extraordinary experience of "dying for Jesus." While psychotic breaks are not common, the themes of them are generally broken into just a few categories. Hearing voices or seeing people from beyond the realm of earth was an obvious example of a break from reality — once I thought about it. The implantation of religious ceremony coupled with the widespread efforts to stretch Christianity made this delusion of becoming a prophet a likely fantasy land to conjure from the outskirts of mental stability within my subconscious.

I didn't know then what would have led me to enact a scene of becoming a prophet. It seemed an odd "hallucination" to have had given my lack of conviction to the Christian stories and its faith. So rather, I believed I met

Jesus just a few short weeks earlier. I didn't think I had been psychotic or that it had been a result of untreated bipolar disorder. I knew something bad happened, but I kept thinking there was an explanation other than a severe mental illness.

I just went to the doctor visits because my brain physically hurt. Mental health professionals were the closest thing on earth that could help me back to whole again, I thought. In a way, I was humoring them. In a way, I was kidding myself. At some level, I knew I had some form of a mood disorder, but I really, really wanted to believe something magical happened to me. I really wanted to believe I was strong enough to eventually leave mental health treatment and draw upon my hardworking, blue collar background and toughen up. There was pride in barging through obstacles unscathed. There was something to be said for surviving adversity. I reasoned that the only reason my brain physically hurt was because I was ripped from my body to crossover to the other side. Healing from this caused headaches. It was like my brain was floating loosely in my skull, I couldn't get it to anchor correctly and function.

"The ability to remember what happens during a psychotic episode is rare. You should let it go," Dr. Burbach said.

I found his advice less than helpful and impossible to follow. The images of the so-called hallucinations remained clear as the delusions lingered convincingly in my mind. Compulsion to unravel this instance of insanity's mystery consumed my days. I tried to hold onto the hallucination as real, because I thought it was the only way to believe my diagnosis of mental illness was false. And I, like many, was conditioned to believe mental health was a pseudo science. No one wants to admit they have a mental health condition. Especially one as feared as bipolar. The stigma surrounding it was and is too great, despite the fact that it affects 2.7 million Americans.

However, the aftermath was so dramatic I had to learn a way to never return to a travel with Jesus or any other hallucination for that matter. I didn't care to meet aliens or whatever other fiction my mind was capable of concocting. I had to let go of Him, and hold just a recollection, and maybe I had to let that memory vanish as well. Maybe Dr. Burbach was right, maybe I needed to let the image of the voyage go or risk returning to the fragile, helpless state. But I wasn't ready.

I wondered why I was meant to go through the humiliation of what they kept calling psychosis. Recovery was degrading as I fumbled my way back to "health" in a maze where I seemed to make progress and then regressed in a whiz of confusion. I couldn't read more than a sentence or two at a time. I couldn't tell time. Some days, my thoughts were coherent, but it tired me to think. I slept a lot and cried and screamed when I was awake. Other days, I lived in a fog where I detached myself from everything optional — small talk, eating. I just did the one thing I had to do: take those damn pills.

The death countdown, my birthday party, Ellen, and the rest of the trip couldn't rationally be explained. I understood this even in my confusion. As a matter of cognition, I realized the episode was not grounded in reality. But I pled, as a matter of respect, that someone would believe the traveling with Jesus really happened — even if only in my mind. It was so vibrant that I couldn't shake its grasp on my own.

"I have to have you believe me. I have to have you understand what happened," I said to Dr. Burbach.

"I know. We're going to help you. You're going to get better. You are going to feel normal again. You have to trust me," he said.

Dr. Burbach gestured to the reference books shelved on top of a file cabinet in his office to the left of his chair. He went on to talk about the research and the diagnostics and other big words. I stopped listening, lost in my thoughts as I tried to think of the next way to communicate what happened. I needed to find a way to make him understand.

"You're going to recover from this," he said.

Recovery was a strange word. It brought to mind the life of an addict, not so much the life of a patient. But I was a patient seeking care from a trio of doctors. That same week I visited Dr. Carducci, the pill dispenser. I meant no disrespect, when I flippantly referred to the pharmaceuticals the psychiatrist supplied in an attempt to bring me back whole. She knew the chemistry of the brain. She knew things she learned in a lifetime of study. She could bring me back to normal. She worked in tandem with my medical doctor to rule out non-mental ailments that may have caused the breakdown. I kept hoping my medical doctor would turn up something other than mania to describe the cause of my mental breakdown, but he never did.

Dr. Burbach began to shift in his seat. I turned to see a mantle clock — glass dome with gold hands — on the end table next to the couch. Looking at it was fruitless, because I couldn't interpret it, but I understood our session had run out of time.

"I want you to make an appointment to see me again in one week," he said. "Jill can help you at the desk."

He was talking to Mike again, not me. That was fine; I was exhausted. I could no longer attempt coherence. We were led back through the hallway to the desk. I hung back behind Mike, who stepped up to the desk and made our next appointment. Mike took care of the details. He did the work. I thought of the Mike on the bike in that Dr. Seuss book. The hills were high.

Alone

Part of my psychiatrist's work was to help me understand reality – to separate the hallucinations — and heal me. Coincidentally, Dr. Carducci shared a practice with her husband Dr. Burbach. Their offices were across the hall from one another. Mike took me to each of them once a week. He backed up what I said to them and provided clarity and credibility, which I couldn't supply on my own regarding my symptoms, setbacks, and strides during this initial recovery phase.

Dr. Carducci was a smart, clever woman who dressed sharply in a sophisticated style. Yet there was a hint of girl next door, because of her approachable personality. She had naturally curly hair that frizzed out of control, yet she slicked it into a barrette and completed her polished look with designer pantsuits or sometimes with pencil skirts.

Since being released into her care, she told me I was her "number one" patient. Mike had the go-ahead to call at any time day or night with concerns regarding me or to report if I was getting worse. She said some people feel special when she names them her number one patient, but I didn't feel special. I was insightful enough to feel scared. I was — pardon me — shitting my pants. When a psychiatrist availed herself to you as her top priority, it could only mean you were skating on the edge of crisis.

Dr. Carducci's work included educating me about my illness; she called it bipolar and probed me for memories of manic episodes in the past similar to the one that escalated to insanity. I thought she probed me to remember the heightened state, but I was not ready to define the behavior which led me to be hospitalized as manic or hypomanic, or worse, admit to a string of them from my personal history. The hospitalization for psychosis was a singular event, and I was not ready to admit that one, I had been psychotic, and two, that it happened because I was bipolar. I went to the psychiatric care center in Green Bay because I believed Mike when he told me I was going to a party. I continued to trust his judgment with the outpatient therapists we selected. I was grateful Mike found a place where I could receive treatment. Yet, I believed the episode of psychosis was a random occurrence, which was isolated, and not part of a larger picture of chronic mental illness. There had to be an explanation other than having bipolar.

I was confused about what was real.

"Meeting Jesus wasn't real," Dr. Carducci said.

I knew Jesus had spoken to me. I understood that no one believed me, and that it was in my best interest to agree with the rest of the world. But seriously, I knew Jesus came to me that night. I wasn't ready to let it go. Real has at least sixteen definitions. I thought Dr. Carducci was using this one: "an actual thing; having objective existence; not imaginary." I pressed on, convinced in my position that Jesus really did visit me and tell me a plan.

"It was real," I told her. "How can you deny what I experienced? I know it was real. It really happened."

"Yes," she concurred. "But it didn't happen on earth, your mind was somewhere else."

I knew she was wrong. I knew Jesus visited me ON EARTH and that I was very much among the living during his visit. I was agitated. Eventually, Dr. Carducci stopped disagreeing with me. She didn't give in, but rather changed the subject. I thought she recognized we weren't making any medical progress debating the merits of real versus imaginary. I was not ready for the truth.

"You are going to get better," she said.

I was about to go off on a stream of the subjective use of the term better.

Instead I asked, "What do you mean by better?"

"Healthier," she said.

Healthier was a word of less ambiguity, which I couldn't argue against. Yet I wondered how a body full of pharmaceuticals was a healthier place.

"It is like someone with diabetes," Dr. Burbach had said at one of my psychotherapy sessions. "Just like a diabetic takes insulin to process blood sugars, people with bipolar can find health with mood stabilizers."

I had raised an eyebrow at this.

"It's different," I had told him.

Of course it was different. It was easy to put mental illness in a category separate from health and box it up as loony. I was programmed not to sympathize with the mentally ill, but rather to laugh at it as a pseudo sickness. And, at all costs, to avoid association with those who were mentally ill. I wasn't alone in that line of thinking: when I told some people what happened, they shushed me; they didn't want to hear about it. They thought mental illness and inpatient therapy was embarrassing and should have been kept private. It was easy to think those afflicted were somehow mentally weak, and they could somehow remove the demon from their brains with enough focus and concentration. That mainstream idea that mental illness was cuckoo thwarted my attempts to accept the diagnosis as grounded in medicine.

"I wish I could tell you about some of the people in the community, who you know, who have bipolar," Dr. Burbach had said once. "With treatment, many people with bipolar are able to live normal, productive lives."

I doubted it. Who were those people and what was normal? I wished I could find and talk to those people. With doctor-patient confidentiality, I was left alone to speculate who these people were, and what their secret was for living productive lives.

I was frustrated by these doctors and the time it was taking for my brain to heal. I was so damn confused. Each time I gathered a piece of insight regarding the diagnosis and treatment, I found more evidence to question if it was true. I read everything I could find about bipolar disorder. I read Kay Redfield Jamison's *An Unquiet Mind: A Memoir of Moods and Madness*. This book scared me when I found pieces in the narrative that looked like me and my symptoms. I found evidence. Bipolar was true, and it was plausible that I had the disease, but not acceptable.

I considered finding a support group, but I couldn't locate any in the rural county where I lived. I would have had to drive 40 miles to attend a support group, and given the fact that I was not allowed to drive this wasn't an option.

So each time I visited Dr. Carducci, she gave Mike instructions and more medications for me. I remained in denial, but I was compliant and took those pills every time they were placed in my palm. I waited, just waited for normal.

Bus Ride

My coffee was waiting for me as I walked into the kitchen after my shower. The pills were there too. There were notes for me as well. Mike hugged me hard, then hugged the boys and left for work. I heard his car start in the driveway and made my way to the window to see him drive past. It was an hour later than he used to leave for work before my breakdown: he had waited for me to get up and dressed. He made sure the boys got dressed, fed them breakfast, and packed their backpacks. His family medical leave time was still approved. He worked nearly full-time with excused time off to take me to my doctor's appointments. I was down to one scheduled each week, alternating between Dr. Burbach and Dr. Carducci; the medical doctor was no longer necessary.

It was my first morning on my own. I was trusted, unsupervised, to take care of myself and my children. I still could not drive. I felt cautiously confident; I wanted to be useful and closer to whole. Joseph, who was in sixth grade, took his bike to school. I decided to take Thomas to school using the city bus. For the boys, I tried to make it sound like an adventure, something fun. Shortly after Mike left, we walked the two blocks to the bus stop. I held each boy's hand, my toddlers flanking my sides as we crossed the busy street. To anyone driving past, we must have looked like normal family, a mom taking a walk with her well-dressed sons. They ran ahead after we crossed the first intersection. I called to them to stop at the next corner when they rushed away from me. I was in control, I thought. My boys were well trained — they listened. They were safety minded and did not run in the road without waiting for me to hold their hands once more.

We arrived early at the bus stop, but I began to panic that I missed the bus. It was supposed to come at 7:50. I still couldn't tell time on a regular clock, so I couldn't wear my gold watch with Roman numerals that Mike had bought me for our first anniversary. My cell phone's digital time was 7:49. The boys asked when the bus was going to come. I tried to hide my own anxiety and reassured them it will be there shortly. They picked dandelions in the terrace.

"These are for you, Momma," Thomas said.

Alex smiled, his blue eyes shining as he looked up at me, and handed me flowers as well. Alex didn't really talk, although he was nearly three. I worried about that. Each of my other boys talked in sentences by that age. Alex made up for his lack of language with an expressive face and subtle gestures. We had him walk and point to what he wanted. I was very good at figuring out what he was trying to "say." It was a game.

The white city bus arrived; the doors opened while the side lowered with a loud sshhh sound. We stepped up; I carried Alex, and Thomas walked ahead of us holding the silver hand rail. The bus was fairly empty. An older woman worked on a crossword puzzle, a pair of cognitively disabled adults smiled vacantly, and a heavy-set black woman looked straight ahead. I took a bench-type seat that faced the aisle. Thomas climbed up, got on his knees and peered through the window as the bus made its way downtown to the transfer station. Alex leaned into me, his face mostly hidden in my chest. At the transfer station, we switched buses to the one that would take us to the north side of town. We disembarked at the stop, which was about five blocks from the school. The boys became tired with the walk. I carried Alex; then Thomas wanted to be carried too, but he had to walk. Several times, he stopped and sat on the sidewalk. I was getting frustrated and urged him to keep walking and assured him we were almost there.

"I never quit, Mom. I just take lots of breaks," he said to me.

I smiled at his tenacity and regained my patience while, at the same time, cursed myself for being so stubborn about thinking I could take the bus. I had been afraid I would forever lose my independence. I wanted to be able to do the simple task of taking my son to school. School started at 8:30 a.m., but there is a grace drop off period starting at 8 a.m.

Finally, we got to the little school at 8:25 a.m. I was sweating and nauseous. I wasn't sure if this was because of the swirl of pills I took before we left the house, or because of motion sickness from the smelly bus, or maybe just walking in the sun, or maybe the aftermath of anxiety. I sat on the school's tyke-sized bench and placed my head between my legs. Thomas made his way to his cubby and changed into his school shoes. Alex stood before me with a concerned look on his face.

"Are you okay?" Thomas's teacher Pam asked me.

"How did you get here?" she asked, noticing the empty parking lot.

"I can't drive. Mike went back to work. I took the bus," I said.

While I still thought in complex ways with an expansive vocabulary, I experienced a detachment from my speech that reduced me to talking simply and slowly. This symptom reminded me of a stroke victim. It was intermittent and came and went. The more stressed I was, the worse my speech. In addition, I also couldn't read a book. When I tried, the text jumbled and I couldn't make out the words; it took a lot of concentration to make out each word at a time and my attention span would expire by the end of a sentence.

This was the first day since my incident that I had been to the school. I had no idea what they knew of my absence: I didn't know if Mike told them or not. He was a pretty private person, so I assumed he hadn't.

"I've been sick," I said. "I am on a lot of medicine, and I can't drive."

"Do you want to go to the bathroom and splash water on your face? Do you want a cup of water?" Pam asked me.

I shook my head.

"I just need a minute," I said.

The bus made its stops every thirty minutes. I had hoped to make it to the school and back to the stop in that time. It looked like I would miss that bus and have to wait for another. Children walked into the lobby looking at me. Alex stayed by my side. A woman, whom I recognized as another parent but did not know by name, stood in the doorway as her son changed his shoes. When she looked at me and looked away, I no longer assumed I looked like a normal mother — I was obviously "out of it." Maybe she and the students saw me as an invalid. I certainly felt like one but refused to be one.

The air was heavy. My mind was foggy. I still felt like I might pass out. It was hard to stay awake; I just wanted to go to sleep. I could barely talk. But I knew I had to get moving, I needed to get Alex home.

"I have to go," I said, and stood on wobbly legs.

I reached for Alex's hand. He took mine. Pam fluttered about.

"Tara, wait, we can have someone drive you home," she said.

I looked around. There was only this one parent here. She avoided eye contact with me.

"Peggy, can you give Tara a ride home?" Pam asked her.

"Where does she live?" Peggy asked, Pam not me.

"Tara, where do you live?" Pam asked me.

"On that street by the church," I said.

Both women looked at each other and then back to me. I lost whatever control I had, I knew I sounded crazy. I couldn't even remember how to recite my address. I tried to pull it together; Alex was counting on me.

"I know how to get there," I said, looking up. "It isn't far."

"Okay, sure," Peggy said.

"Great," Pam said.

"What about him?" Peggy asked, gesturing to Alex.

Technically, Alex was old enough to attend the preschool. The Montessori school accepted children from age 2 through kindergarten. However, we decided to keep him home for another year. Pam stalled for minute, looking back from me to Alex to Peggy.

"Tara, can you take care of Alex?" she asked.

I remembered Dr. Carducci saying that I could. I nodded.

"Can you take both of them?" Pam looked back to Peggy, who shrugged.

"Does he have a car seat?" she asked.

Jesus, I was getting annoyed, but was careful not to become "agitated." Clearly, this woman didn't expect to be taking home a complete stranger. As the time passed, I started to feel a little better. My stomach settled. I was no longer afraid motion would make me puke.

"It is okay. I can take the bus. Alex, it is time to take another walk," I said, trying hard to keep my voice cheerful.

Pam looked at Peggy.

"He can fit in Caden's car seat," Pam said.

"Um okay, sure," Peggy said.

150

She bent over to give her son a hug. Thomas was long gone from the entryway, having made his way to the classroom. Pam looked at me.

"Peggy will take you and Alex home," she said.

I nodded and followed Peggy to her newer model Jeep Liberty. It was black and nice. My own vehicle was a blue Dodge Grand Caravan with over 100,000 miles. Technically, Alex was too small to safely ride in the older boy's car seat. But Peggy put him in it and adjusted the straps. It seemed clear to me she was uncomfortable with the arrangement, but maybe that was just my self-consciousness again.

"I'm Tara," I said.

"I'm Peggy. We met at the children's museum a few months ago," she said.

Shit, I didn't remember that. I was uncomfortable and felt like I owed this woman some sort of explanation.

"I'm sorry. I don't remember that. You see. I had a nervous breakdown. Well, I guess they call it a psychotic break. My memory isn't very clear," I said. "I have a hard time with talking."

She said nothing in return. So, I filled the space with more confessions.

"I guess I have bipolar. So that's what they think caused it. I was in the hospital. I see three doctors. They have me on a lot of medicine," I said.

She didn't react as if I told her I was clinically insane. She acted like I just told her I had a root canal. She told me to buckle up and made her way out of the parking lot, turning left toward town.

"Where do you live?" she asked.

"You go this way, we aren't far," I said.

She was very calm as I figured out where to turn and found my street. She pulled into our long, narrow driveway and stepped out of the car to get Alex out of the seat behind her. I walked around the car and took Alex by the hand.

"Thanks for the ride," I said.

"Do you have to get Thomas at 11:30?" she asked.

Oh yeah, I thought, how was I going to do that? I nodded.

"Yeah, I'll take the bus. I bought a monthly pass. My stomach is better now," I said, trying to sound tough.

"If you bring me a car seat for him, I can drop him off for you," she said.

I was skeptical. This woman said very little to me in the car ride home. She seemed nice though. I was both grateful and embarrassed by her offer. And honestly, this was a time when I needed help. And I felt bad asking Mike to take more time from work. Reluctantly, I made my way to my van and pulled out the car seat. It was sticky and dirty, so I used my hand to dust it off. Her car was so clean and nice; I was afraid what she would think when she saw this car seat. I walked back to her car and found her playing with Alex in the front yard. I handed her the car seat, which she put into her Jeep without making any indication that she was judging the state it was in.

"Are you going to be okay with this guy?" she asked, referring to my youngest.

"Yeah, we'll go in. Watch some cartoons," I said. "My doctor said it is fine that I take care of him."

"Well, here's my number. If you need anything, you can call me. I don't have to work today," Peggy said.

"Okay," I said, knowing I wouldn't call.

I walked with Alex to the front door. She pulled out of the driveway. Inside, I set up PBS cartoons and laid on the couch, then fought to stay awake. Alex played with toys on the area rug in the center of the living room. I got up and got a glass of water for myself and filled a sippy cup of chocolate milk for Alex. He was a good toddler, happy. He sat quietly on the floor.

Get Well Soon

For weeks, I continued to feel a physical fragileness in my brain. It felt like a healing scab that itches as it forms on a scraped knee. My brain tingled as it worked toward becoming fully functioning again. I hoped the scar tissue that remained was strong enough to protect my brain from another awful betrayal of self. Mike said I was hesitant in my mannerisms. I could see little progress, yet I was allowed to drive at low speeds. I knew what day it was: The Google calendar printed and hanging on the refrigerator helped me know what needed to be done each day. Most days were free of scheduled activities, except those regular doctor visits. The medical doctor only saw me once, performed a battery of lab tests, and confirmed that I have hypothyroidism and likely bipolar disorder. He refilled the Synthroid prescription that I had been taking since my thyroid problem was discovered years earlier.

Dr. Carducci had given me a timeline of six to eight weeks to regain normal life. I lost days of life and memory while spending time in recovery at the psychiatric center. I was told I was admitted on Monday, March 29, 2010, around noon and was released late afternoon on Good Friday, April 2: just five days of inpatient therapy. If the forecast of my healing was correct, I should have returned to "health" by mid-May.

It was then mid-May, and I was not normal yet. I was still clumsy and still exhibited rage, but mostly I felt as if I walked in a fragile fog. I dressed myself, even wore some makeup and styled my hair. I could read again for short periods, though some days this took more effort and caused headaches. For all the fixing up on the outside, however, I could not shake the feeling of unrest inside. I didn't feel as though I belonged anywhere. I did not feel sane. I wondered if I would continue in this fog indefinitely. While I wasn't an invalid any longer, I also wasn't fully functioning and, therefore, I still depended on Mike.

I resumed my three classes at UW Green Bay. These were online courses, and I was given until the end of summer to complete them. My concentration was limited, and I could only work on them for short periods of time.

Dr. Carducci had told me I was getting better as she continued to modify the doses and varieties of medication at each visit. I let Mike take care of getting them from the pharmacy, paying for them, and administering them to me. I had an alarm to remind me take them when he was not home. Dr. Carducci also told me, just as Dr. Burbach had, there was no value in naval gazing and trying to remember. I decided, early on, I never wanted to return to what the professionals were classifying as a psychotic state. However, to forget was to pretend it was not real, and I was not ready to admit I didn't meet Jesus. I prayed a lot, which both my mental health physicians encouraged. I held strongly a belief something divine existed.

"There is only so much science can explain," I said at one visit. "I have to believe in a higher power to answer the rest."

"Yes, we are working under those same assumptions," Dr. Burbach said. "Spirituality is helpful for your treatment."

My mind held images of the planets, solar systems, and galaxies situated in a cosmic blur. I also remembered the picture of earth taken from space on that puzzle at the psychiatric center. I saw myself as a mere pin needle on the vast landscape of the abyss; I was nothing more than a collection of atoms. Feeling insignificant, I held a deep hunger to find something to make myself feel useful and relevant.

I started treatment on a schedule of Geodon, but Dr. Carducci changed that medication to Lamictal. I didn't know the difference and hadn't bothered too much with reading the information labels that came tucked in the pharmacy's paper bags. I occasionally searched Google and longed to be rid the pills. I feared the side effects, yet the fear of psychosis always trumped the possible side effects of those pills I continued to swallow throughout the day. I also took Abilify, an antipsychotic, which is sometimes prescribed as an antidepressant. I took Lorazepam as needed; the need was undefined, but it was for the general category of anxiety. I used it whenever I felt agitated or overwhelmed. I took Lorazepam every morning, every time I was about to enter a crowd, and when I felt an argument coming on with Mike. As the pill dissolved on my tongue, I felt it calm my blood, which felt bubbly enough to cause my skin to tingle. I compared the little pill to a glass of wine that worked in less than five minutes and didn't sour my breath. It relaxed me in a way I've never achieved without it. It allowed me to stop fidgeting and really observe the world around me. I could step back and assess without feeling the need to explain, interact, or control.

"We want you to get well," Dr. Carducci said, as a way to reassure me that we were on the cusp of pinpointing the right combination of chemicals that would enable me to live mostly free of bipolar's symptoms.

I didn't want to believe the evidence and accept that I had bipolar, especially since I was frustrated that I was not normal yet, even though I complied to every experiment with medications Dr. Carducci supplied. I was on a medical leave of absence from work; worse, it was unclear if I would ever return. As a mobility manager, I was charged with improving the efficiency, availability, and access to transportation services for the most vulnerable citizens, namely the elderly, disabled, and poor. Ironically, the mentally ill also fill a space of those vulnerable clients who relied on public transportation. And sadly, I was desperately ill and very vulnerable. Yet, I was lucky. I was not abandoned, and I was blanketed in a place of middle-class medicine, which gave me some hope.

I spent my days as a stay-at-home mother. I kept Alex with me when we went outside. I kept him out of the danger of the busy street, didn't allow him to run with sticks, made sure he had wore sunscreen, and had plenty to drink. Thomas attended school in the mornings. It was hard to remember to pick him up on time... Sometimes, I was late. The Montessori school owner Pam knew what I had been through; she was kind and compassionate. She kept Thomas safe when I was late, and never judged me or charged me for the wraparound childcare. I had a strong, support team to take care of me and my family.

My husband was a nearly omnipresent source of comfort who shouldered the bulk of demands of maintaining our household while coordinating my health care. He was the person lucid enough to oversee my health care and the family. My parents visited and took my children to their home. Carol provided a continuous stream of support in the way of groceries, childcare, cleaning, inspirational note cards, and friendship. And support came in the form of phone calls from my old friend Heather, my neighbor's couch to sit on when I needed an escape from the family, my friend Catherine's kitchen table of conversations; and an invitation for a walk through the park from my Uncle Tony. My sister Billie called me and told me she prayed for me.

My mother-in-law was the only person thoughtful enough to send flowers. Others answered phone calls. But no one sent a card to me in the hospital or at home afterwards.

If I had been in an accident, I'd have received flowers, candies, or balloons; but since my health problems were mental in nature, people didn't know how to react. I didn't blame them. If someone I knew had suffered a nervous breakdown, I'd have stayed away and allowed them to recover in privacy from such an embarrassing sickness. I probably would have thought this person simply lost their marbles and needed time alone to pull it back together. After having been subjected to the humiliation of a mental breakdown, I learned comfort and help was appreciated and necessary.

As I recovered at home, a few people — like ambulance chasers — came, eager to hear and see what had happened. A handful of people closest to me offered solace in a period of confusion. Many more people looked the other way and tended to their own lives. I could only speculate what kept people away. Probably, it had less to do with me and more to do with their own lives — jobs, kids, stress, etc. I also suspected it was because mental illness was not widely accepted as a sickness. It was not a "disease" in the physical sense. Its maladies were not recognizable from a blood test or X-ray. Maybe someday, with brain imaging, society would be able to recognize mental illness as a physical ailment affecting the brain. Until then, those afflicted had to put their faith in a group of doctors, who were not always respected by the mainstream. These medical professionals were disrespected with terms such as "quack" and "shrink." Even I couldn't accept the legitimacy of mental illness. Mom suggested I take up yoga again, as if a series of sun salutations could heal me from the insanity that overcame me. There was too much uncertainty surrounding mental illness to accept the category as 100 percent valid.

It was hard to look in its face and say, "I care about you. I understand you. I believe you are real."

Mental illness was hidden behind the murkiness of doubt's shadows. As a result, people simply didn't know what an appropriate response was when psychosis struck and hurt a person. Many people didn't recognize it as an injury — as for me, I thought of my nervous breakdown as a traumatic brain injury. My mother-in-law's flowers with a stemmed card signed simply with her name signified someone's hope that I would recover. The gesture of kindness reminded me to seek health and "Get Well." I was grateful for the consideration my disease was given. I called her and told her as much.

Writing Friend

Mike continued calling me an artist. He considered my writing artful and encouraged me to work at it. My doctors echoed his recommendation, and thought writing could help me achieve health.

I imagined an artist as a peaceful creator who sees the world and walks delicately through it, observing nature with fresh eyes. This was not at all how I saw myself. I saw myself as an unstable, emotional wreck, residing in an overweight body. I saw a person who was scared and distractible, unable to commit to the craft, uncertain of my worth. Regarding my vocational purpose, I teeter tottered between a sensible pursuit (a full-time job) and a lofty ambition (a career as an author) when considering what to do with my life. As a result, I self inflicted paralysis and didn't do either effectively. I started a track with gumption, then freaked out and picked the other path. I had the luxury of time for honing my craft, but squandered it on naps and vices.

Maybe Mike saw me as an artist, because I was sensitive, observant, and sometimes witty. I dug out some of my old writing, poems, short stories, and the half-finished great American novel. I checked out writing magazines and books from the library. I reread Anne Lamott's *Bird by Bird: Some Instructions on Writing and Life* and Steven King's *On Writing: A Memoir of the Craft*. I found writing communities online and a state writing conference, which was being held in my hometown.

There was a poetry reading Friday night of the conference, and since I was preoccupied with becoming a poet laureate, I decided to go and share some of my work. I discarded the teenage-angst ones, and brought those, which I thought were mature and strong. I read them; they were not heavily applauded. I left there not feeling defeated, but rather inspired to improve my voice and write better poetry.

The following day, I watched a brief performance of a screen play. I heard speakers on publishing, marketing, and writing in general. Then it was lunch, which was held in a different area of the convention center. I walked up to the buffet line, filled my plate with a sandwich, some fresh fruit, and a salad. In my other hand, I held my silverware and a cup of coffee. I entered the dinning call, and saw most of the seats taken and no one had food yet. It was then, I realized it was proper to find a seat and wait for the wait staff to release the tables one by one to travel though the buffet line. My face turned red, the heat of embarrassment caused me to sweat. I slowly moved in a circle, searching for an empty seat. I wanted to drop my plate and run out of the room, hoping to avoid crying until I got to my van or at least the parking lot.

Thankfully, a beautiful woman with kind, brown eyes, and perfect soft, long brown hair caught my eye and smiled at me. She gestured to an empty seat at her round table. I sighed a relief and joined the group. I gushed apologies for my social faux pas of getting my food first. They all assured me it was an honest mistake and no big deal. Amanda introduced herself and her father, and the rest of the table. These were the members of the local writing group: Minds without Boundaries. She invited me to join them the following Saturday.

I did. I read a piece that would become a chapter of this book. They were silent. I read about waking up in the psychiatric care center, lost and confused. The room was quiet. They eventually filled the awkward gap of silence with encouraging words. I was not sure if they really respected the writing or recognized how fragile I was. I needed confirmation that I should continue to write my story.

I attended the meetings regularly, gaining insight on writing a memoir and improving my work. I found much talent among the group and a safe place to be an artist. It was at this time, that I started to transition from seeing myself as a hack, and rather as an artist. I felt worthy of filling the pages in the journal Mike gifted me in the hospital.

Days, from then on, included at least an hour of writing. Bit by bit, or bird by bird, I wrote. I believed the final product would become a memoir. I thought it could have value, because mental health memoirs were too often told from the perspective of a family member or celebrity, leaving the story of the afflicted up to a reader's imagination. I thought I had something to add to the conversation of mental illness, and I wanted there to be a dialogue.

Jesus Freak

I remained convinced that committing to a higher power was the only way to recover from my insanity. So, I reached for those people in my life, who had openly accepted Jesus as their own savior and who worked evangelically to recruit others to salvation. Those people closest to me were genuinely and sensibly concerned about my well-being, and they need me to let the story of meeting Jesus go. However, I needed to hold onto any truth that existed in the hallucination, so I sought out my fringe friends who I knew held a conviction to Christ.

With faith, I thought, maybe I could rid the medications from my body. Maybe I could have gained the strength to walk on my own. Meanwhile, Dr. Carducci was smart enough to tell me to just take the pills for one more month; she was careful to not say for the rest of my life. Maybe I could be healed.

I wanted to go to church. Some Sundays I made it a Catholic Mass. Sometimes, I attended a nondenominational church, but those churches never felt right to me. I preferred the ritual and predictability of Mass. I didn't like feeling desperate. I considered nondenominational churches for failures who were lost and who first came to know Christ later in life. I had had the benefit of a Catholic upbringing and was familiar with the story of Christ. The faith-free-wave-your-hands-in-the-air churches seemed a mockery of the sanctuaries where I was familiar and comfortable.

My sister Billie, despite having attended the same Wednesday night Catechism classes as me, came to Christ late in life, dunking herself in a river with a slew of new believers. I considered the Catholic version of the Apostles Creed, which I learned and recited for years, to be true: only one baptism was recognized for the forgiveness of sins. So I found my sister's new faith illogical, especially the part of being born again or re-baptized.

She went to church in a theater-type building. I took my great grandfather there one Christmas Eve for service. When the stage filled with jolly women dressed in red sweaters dancing with jazz hands and tossing peppermint candies to the crowd while singing "Joy to the World," the then 90-year-old man stood up and said, "This isn't church. This is a God-damn theater."

I shared his sentiments as well as appreciated the irony of his statement. But I settled him into "enjoying the show" with a promise of Midnight Mass later in the evening.

Now I looked for those people who worshiped in the privacy of their homes. I looked for those who had dismissed the rituals and dogma of organized religion, because I also felt all religion was a manmade construct and therefore short of divinity. Still, I wanted to be a Christian. I wanted to believe in Jesus Christ as the son of God. However, given the distortion of Christ I witnessed in what I was told was psychosis, this was difficult.

A woman, who was the mother of a friend of a friend, was so moved when hearing of my ailment she asked me if she could pray with me at a child's birthday party. My two young sons were in the care of other party guests when I agreed to pray with her. I was uncomfortable praying with strangers in non-church settings, but I didn't want to be rude. Besides, I believed prayer could help, so I welcomed her pure gesture and followed her to a back bedroom. She prayed:

"Dear Heavenly Father, I come to you today with your child, Tara. She is hurting, Lord. She has been tricked by

Satan to believe in the man-made lie of mental illness. Please put your arms around her and bring her to peace. Lord, we ask that you protect Tara and keep her healthy and strong. Help her to get off the drugs these doctors are prescribing, which are making her worse. Help her to find real strength and courage in your arms, Lord. We ask this through your son, Jesus Christ."

While she said the prayer, she had closed her eyes and rested her hands on my shoulders. This woman nearly shook me, but really, it was more of a gentle rocking back and forth to soothe my attention into the prayer.

"Tara, you have to believe. You have to accept Jesus as your Savior. You have to say this now," the stranger said.

I started to explain that I had accepted Jesus as my savior long ago in a white dress as I prepared to take a serving of the body of Christ at my First Communion ceremony, which was held in a rural Catholic Church.

She vehemently shook her head.

"No, those are lies," she said. "Satan disguises himself in things you think are good."

She waited quietly as I began to grow more uncomfortable and looked for a door or way out of the situation. I didn't want to tell this woman she was cuckoo, but the exercise seemed irrational. Yet, I was close enough to my hospital release and still stuck in denial of the bipolar and not yet healthy. I decided to hear what she had to say. Once my attention focused again, she continued.

"Tara, you have to do what Jesus wants of you. You have to accept him as your Savior and live according to His rules. You have to give up the man-made lies. Are you ready to pray with me?"

Not seeing much of a choice, I agreed to pray with her, thinking it would make her feel like a good soldier of the Lord. I also grasped at the chance that submitting myself in prayer would help me navigate away from prescriptions. She fed me line by line, and I dutifully repeated each segment.

I prayed, "Lord, on this day,"

"I accept Jesus as my Lord and Savior."

"I ask you for guidance, as I grow in my path toward health."

"Please help me along my way."

"I am your faithful child."

"Amen."

When I left the gathering that day, I didn't feel any less crazy. I didn't feel healed. As much as I denied my diagnosis, it felt unnatural to abandon intellect and research to blindly have faith in Jesus Christ as the one and only answer to end my suffering.

Sometime after this encounter, I vaguely told another evangelical friend out of context "I met Jesus Christ."

She nodded encouragingly, her confirming gestures implying that indeed I met the Savior. She didn't have the experience of having been a cherub child oiled and bathed in holy clothing at baptism; instead, she too immersed herself in a river of baptism with other adults who held a conviction of being born again in Christ. Encouragement to trust only Christ to heal a medical problem was given without realizing the harm of holding the delusions. Allowing me to delay progress by reaching for some spiritual vision in the hallucination crippled the work the doctors were doing.

I thought of a recent news story about an 11-year-old girl who died of a diabetic complication in central Wisconsin. Her parents had put their faith in God to heal her rather than consulting a doctor who could easily treat her with insulin to keep her alive. They believed her death was God's will. By doing nothing in the eyes of the law and medical community, they eventually were convicted of wrongful death.

If my Christian friends only knew the harm they caused by delaying my treatment, they wouldn't have carried on at the edge of their seats waiting for more morsels of Gospel-affirming events in my insanity. They had been so quick to grasp my insanity as a rational visit with the Lord Jesus Christ, rather than putting me and my caricature of Jesus in the same category as those who heard voices or claimed they had seen aliens. The denial allowed me to consider the disease false. However, in order to treat a problem, it must be recognized and accepted as problematic. The denial kept me from believing that I could be both well and bipolar. I denied bipolar thinking that the only way to be healthy was the absence of a mental illness. I didn't yet understand that one could be simultaneously happy, healthy, product, normal even while treating a chronic illness.

Perhaps if I had talked about the sterile walls at the care center where I was treated and remembered that place more vividly than the hallucination, I wouldn't have enticed my Christian friends to consider the experience holy or spiritual. These Christian friends did not know the rest of the story, either: they did not know the depths of sickness that was managed in the care of scientific, medical professionals at the psychiatric center and the staff at Lakeview Psychological Associates.

It is worth noting here that my sister, while a born-again Christian, was not part of the group of people I sought for spiritual intervention. Billie was a big supporter of treatment.

Nervous Breakdown

By late June, I regained more of my independence but was advised to avoid stress. Mike indulged me, letting me find simple pleasures of life. I went for walks. I baked cookies. I wrote in that journal he purchased for me. I spent time at the library.

And, as it was summer, I went to community festivals, parks, and the farmers' market. One Saturday morning, I ran into a cousin at the market in downtown Manitowoc, which was staged in a parking lot adjacent to the mouth of the Manitowoc River with Lake Michigan visible on the horizon. There were about seventy booths of produce, crafts, and prepared festival foods.

"How are you?" my cousin asked.

I sensed she knew of my mental breakdown, but I decided to keep the exchange light.

"I am doing better and feeling good," I said.

"So you had a nervous breakdown?" she asked.

I nodded and looked away from her, still ashamed at this fact. I remained convinced everyone thought I was mentally weak. I couldn't her and use the correct medical terminology for my condition. I remained afraid of considering myself psychotic or having experienced a weeklong stretch of psychosis. So, I chose to refer to this episode in my life as a nervous breakdown. It sounded vaguer, and, as a result, it was almost romantic in its interpretation. I hated to think of the looks from faces I saw when I told people "psychotic break," which I imagined conjured up notions of a deranged and dangerous psycho — though this horrific glance would have offered a more accurate processing of what I experienced. A nervous breakdown is something people sometimes say, though not usually in referring to clinical insanity, as in "I think I'm going to have a nervous breakdown" or "I'm going crazy" when feeling overwhelmed. My psychotic episode was traumatic and tragic, but also it became a gateway for understanding my lack of place and rest in this world.

"Turns out I can't do it all. I'm not superwomen," I told her, trying to keep the conversation light and avoid a full-on confession of the chaos of psychosis and the pain that followed.

We laughed together about the stress of managing work, children, and marriage. She asked about my marriage; I had publicly announced my frustration with the marriage that spring on Facebook.

"It wasn't really Mike. It was me. I wasn't well. He's been a saint through all of this," I admitted.

People weaved around us carrying canvas shoulder bags overflowing with produce. Some slurped blended bubble tea drinks and others ate egg rolls wrapped in grease-trapped napkins.

"Some days I feel like I'm going to have a nervous breakdown," she confided. "With running two businesses and my kids, I just feel like I can't keep up. You know?"

I nodded again as a way to validate her feelings. Feelings of becoming overwhelmed are something we all encounter. But the thing that separated my cousin's experience from my own was I didn't feel like I was having a nervous breakdown. In the weeks and months leading up to the disastrous crash of self into insanity, I felt better than ever.

"I honestly didn't feel like I was going to have one. It came as a surprise, completely unexpected," I said.

This statement signaled the end of the conversation and we wrapped up catching up on family gossip such as pregnancies, engagements, and marital separations.

Lexicon Station

Knowing what was crazy, uncontrolled mania and what was logical ambition was difficult to distinguish in the time following the breakdown. I needed to live in an environment as free from stress as possible. Meanwhile, I had a houseful of boys, chronic, unscheduled days, as well as the anxiety surrounding my recovery from a psychotic break and the subsequent medical presumption of bipolarity.

I took care of my children. I dabbled in landscaping. Well, really not landscaping, but rather clearing the rocks from the shrubs in front of our house. These rocks were not burnt red pebbles or evenly-shaped white rocks, but rather jagged, mismatched, hideous rocks. I decided to remove them from around the seven evergreen shrubs bordering the entrance of our home. I gathered five-gallon pails and each day I sat in the front yard collecting those rocks from their bed and plunking them into the pails. I was determined and focused on the task alone. I had no vision for what would become of the space once the rocks were removed; I just wanted them gone. This task took on almost a compulsive nature.

Another part of reducing the stress in my life was the direct order to not return to work. Before the breakdown, I had been working under a year-long contract in a suburban county just north of Milwaukee. My doctors had advised that the ramifications of revealing a mental illness could devastate a career; I should request a medical leave of absence. Against the advice of my physicians, I told my contract supervisor everything that had happened to me. Before taking me out to lunch, my boss asked me to sign a document terminating my contract. I did follow the advice to not sign anything, and told her as much. She was unfazed and accepted a verbal agreement that I would not return.

I finally had the opportunity to do nothing. I had never felt like I fit in anywhere in the world and work was my biggest struggle. I needed to find a career, eventually. I was not going to remain content with dependence on another to support me financially, though Mike's arms were strong enough to do so.

So I looked at this medical leave of absence as an opportunity to explore the life I wanted to live. By then, I read and wrote compulsively. My favorite subject to write about was the travels with Jesus. I thought if I wrote it enough ways, in poems or fiction or essay, it would become valid and true and in some way undo the diagnosis, undo the psychotic history.

I also kept a journal of goals and plans. Considering myself a writer, but realizing the reality of becoming a published author was more than a long shot (I had never finished writing a book), I decided to put my energies into establishing a gathering place where writers would come to garner inspiration for the craft. Of course, these places in some fashion already existed. There were coffee shops and libraries and book stores where writers found themselves a nook. Big-box stores and office-supply stores sold the tools needed for the craft. Yet, I thought there was a niche market to create a unique space devoted exclusively to writers. I believed in a business opportunity combining workshops and retail and coffee.

I toyed with the idea of opening a retail shop called "Lexicon Station." Lexicon was a rip off from the PBS cartoon, Word Girl, whose character comes from the planet Lexicon. Lexicon also was a resource of categorization of words. Station was reminiscent of a gas station where writers could refuel.

The dream was to have a place where writers could find both solace and camaraderie; the retail end was selling paper and pens. The store would have carried novelty items, muses I supposed. Another area would have been devoted to used books about the craft. What else writers needed, at least in my mind, was coffee, wine, and simplistic non-messy foods, which would be available at a counter. Small tables encouraging one to sit alone and work would be positioned around the room. The store also would have had a large round or oval table to host writing circles, critique groups, and workshops, because as solitary as the craft seems, camaraderie and bona fide connectivity with like-minded sorts was paramount to success in my mind.

That was my idea. I wasn't sure if it was realistic, given my lack of capital to get it started as well as the lack of confidence to trust myself. But my husband supported the idea enough to allow me to plan; he bought, on credit, a new laptop, the latest Microsoft software, and QuickBooks.

Because the name of the business was terrible really, I moved on to calling it "Paper & Pen" and then played with the idea of calling it "Pen & Ink." I spent an exuberant amount of time distracting myself with what to call this place, and in between I went to "work" to find a way to make it a reality. I went so far as to have my MBA husband write Performa reports and together we looked at buildings for sale and for lease. A friend even designed a Web site and logo for the business. I was serious, but the idea never became anything more than an idea. I found there was no market for such a place in our blue collar community. It would have drained both me and our finances. So I was left to wonder if it was a grandiose idea, that word I heard was associated with mania. At least, my brain had started to think again. At least I could plan and after the exploration, I was able to recognize it was not a worthwhile pursuit.

I thought about my time in the hospital and how I nearly died — really it was a near-death experience in my assessment. I thought there was a finite amount of time on earth and we must find a way to produce the life we were meant to live. So my authentic pulse was returning; I just couldn't completely breathe on my own. But I was fortunate to have this luxury of support to help me get the oxygen back to my cells and the person I was back to self-efficacy.

Finding Mania

As awful as the idea of a serious mental illness is, I climbed onboard, but was afraid to believe it completely. By this point, I had accepted psychosis and depression as mental illnesses as acute instances in my past. I drew a line in the sand: I didn't want to believe the bipolar part. This disease, formerly called manic depressive, seemed way worse in severity than the others, and it was chronic, unending. I wanted to be saved from a lifetime wrought with depression and the destruction that it caused, but I denied mania. I was afraid the doctors were wrong, and worried their additional mental tinkering with medications would leave my brain more damaged and susceptible to early-onset Alzheimer's, schizophrenia, or worse — death at my own hands. I feared that acceptance of bipolar disorder would bring me to a place of lifelong mental illness. I was not ready to be what I then considered chronically crazy. So I took the medicine one dose at a time. I swallowed the pills and hoped it was a temporary fix.

"I think you are getting better," Dr. Carducci assured me at every visit.

The crux of the matter was, in order for me to get better, I had to recognize the mania had to be present. I had to find it. According to the field of study, just one incident of mania was all that was needed to diagnose bipolar. I realized that the months leading up to my psychotic break were diagnosable as mania. That wasn't enough for me — I wanted to find further validation of the disease bipolar. I didn't agree one incident was enough to deserve the chronic bipolar label, and I kept hoping it was a blip, some sort of mistake.

Sometimes we can't see what is right in front of us. Some people with bipolar embrace their mania and forgo treatment just to have tastes of excessiveness. As for me, I embraced depression as a manageable condition, where I could remove myself from society by covering myself in bed until the symptoms "cleared up." I pushed the reality of the mania deep in denial. I never thought the mania was present, much less a problem, or, much more pragmatic, a symptom of mental illness. Manic was a strong word, hypomanic was less severe and probably the symptom that most often balanced the depression in my life. Hypomanic is a word Dr. Carducci introduced to me.

The doctors' use of these words, mania and hypomania, I didn't really understand. I looked them up. Wikipedia became my bible, as I longed to understand what these words meant and how they related to me.

I learned hypomania is a less severe form of mania. Hypomania is a mood that many don't perceive as a problem, because it feels good to have numerous accomplishments, especially after long stretches of unproductive depression. While hypomanic, one has a greater sense of well-being and productivity. Ideas come fast. Sometimes, though, hypomania can evolve into mania.

Mania is when ideas start coming too fast and there are too many to process. In this stage of the symptom, confusion replaces clarity and the juggling balls begin to fall. Perception is greatly distorted. All the rage episodes in my history were comingled with mania, and sadly a result of distorted impression of reality where I felt justified in my outbursts. A person with mania can begin to lose touch with reality. It isn't just excessive spending, crazy partying, grandiose ideas, although those are also included. It is the intensity and illogical actions.

I first found hypomania in a journal. I always wrote. Mostly, these writings were personal journals that chronicled the struggles of my life. I rarely wrote when happy, or maybe I was rarely happy. I wrote poems: some were profound; most were trite.

Also among my writing were boxes of clips from the five years I worked as a newspaper reporter. As I looked for clues to this mental illness the professionals were saying I had, these stores of narration seemed a good place to start.

I pulled out five heavy boxes of clips from the basement and stacked them in our breakfast nook in the back of our kitchen where there was a small table for two, which generally held my laptop. We didn't eat in this space; it had become my makeshift office. This set-up created a mess in our living space and I worried that it bothered Mike. Mike was mellow; he never said it bothered him. In fact, he was supportive and reassured me that I could do anything I wished.

I began to look through the news clips for some insight. I looked for it more to disprove the bipolar theory more than to find a way to accept mania. Finding it would have confirmed the doctor's diagnosis and confirmed that I really did have bipolar, which is a severe mental illness. Not finding it, after a good-faith search of my personal history, would have meant sanity and an improper diagnosis from the medical staff. Mental illness was a sickness, but I couldn't see that: all I saw was crazy. I wanted to find out how I landed in the hospital, and if these doctors who claimed to be leading me to health were wrong in their diagnosis. I was sure to find them wrong.

The yellowing newspaper clippings sparked some good memories but didn't reveal any clues of mania. The beauty of writing news was the writer, herself, was hidden behind someone else's stories. Each time I went on assignment I was like the wallflower at the middle school dance, watching the events unfold. Even the commentaries lacked a first-person point of view, because they were hidden behind a narrator. I didn't have to participate. I could judge and question and summarize. I could write without risk of revealing myself. So as I sifted through the clips, none of my own stories were found. I marveled at some of my stronger pieces, and then I moved on to the manila folder of thank you cards. It was about four inches thick of cards and printed emails. I saved every positive affirmation I received.

Bobbie V., a photojournalist who was miffed by the corporate culture that invaded the sacred newsroom, pooh-poohed the value of these thank you cards that I coveted. He received many thank you cards for the images he captured around the community. But rather than keeping them, he'd toss the cards in the recycling bin saying, "This and a $1.67 will get me a loaf of bread at the grocery store."

Gratitude was free to give and nothing to receive, Bobbie thought. It didn't get deposited into a cash account and couldn't be bartered for goods. I, however, thrived on the thank you card. I needed the affirmation that someone thought I was worthwhile in order to continue the work. I needed to believe I was talented, and the only measure I could find was collecting those dang thank you cards.

Searching through the thank you cards built my self-esteem but, again, didn't reveal any hint of mania. I craved validation and received it hundreds of times, but still couldn't believe I had any worthwhile qualities. Certainly a person with mania would be able to find it couched in accomplishments. But that isn't where I found it. Mania was more destructive than depression ever was to me; I just didn't know it then.

What I thought I knew of mania was that it was a blissful place. I couldn't remember reaching "bliss" ever. The idea that I ever experienced the opposite of depression was baffling to me. The doctors must have been wrong, I thought. I couldn't have a bipolar disorder, like they kept saying at each of my appointments, because I've never had an elevated mood. What I knew of mania was wrong — it was based on information garnered from the media portrayals of the symptom. I thought bipolar involved highs and lows, and knowing that the pendulum in my brain only swung from low to normal — never high — I was sure I didn't experience any mania. But mania is also an exaggeration of grand thinking. It is racing thoughts and impulsivity, and can manifest itself as rage or agitation as well as joy. It is an exponential multiplier of an elevated mood that carries with it distortions of reality. In the chaos of delusions, destruction can occur. This destruction has manifested itself in the forms of humiliation and rage more than once in my life.

The household was sleeping; it was early morning, probably 5 a.m. I pulled out a journal that was kept during my days as a college student. I took colored markers and circled those entries containing good writing, and then circled or underlined in a different color the passages where I found evidence of the disease. Depression, suicidal thoughts, etc. were there repeatedly, but still no mania.

Sometimes the prose included pictures or sketches. Sometimes, my penmanship became frantic. This change in penmanship indicated I had lapsed into a trance of stream of conscious writing. The words recorded in this special penmanship were utterly poetic and revealing of universal truisms, I had thought as they were recorded. As a more seasoned writer, I realized these were just cathartic writing, not wisdom. One such example was so profound that after I wrote it, I had copied it onto a piece of stationary and mailed it to a hometown friend. She had said then that she didn't understand it.

She was gentle, not wanting to upset me, when she said, "Tara, this doesn't make any sense."

I didn't realize at the time the writing didn't make any sense. The jumbled mess of musings didn't record a coherent thought. It was nonsense. I had just thought then my friend wasn't as gifted as me to be able to reach this higher level of understanding. Looking at it that morning with the colored markers, I realized she was right: the passage of wonderment was crazy. It didn't make any sense.

This was the first example of racing thoughts and unclear thinking I located:

I'm doing better than the day before everyday simply because I appreciate the good things and remember the knowledge obtained on that day. I feel that every day I'm one step closer to figuring "it" all out. I will be stepping for the rest of my life, but I'm still not clear on what I'm stepping toward. It is a complicated series of whatever that makes me who I am and makes everybody else who they are too. I want to figure out the "me" part of it before I can figure out the "they" part of "it." But just knowing that "it" exists, helps me to understand the "me" part of "it." All my life, I've seen and heard and lived puzzle pieces and I am understanding why. I think I have the border down now and it's up to me to fill in the middle with experiences and people that I choose. I can create a beautiful puzzle and I will make this my goal.

What an embarrassment to realize that one, I had written this, and two, I had thought it was good stuff. It was written in the special penmanship that signaled to me that I was really getting somewhere. I didn't cry as I read it, but sighed defeated. I was recognizing hypomania, and that I had it, as I saw an actual record of my own racing, disconnected thoughts. More frightening was the belief I held that this was talent to record such universal wisdom.

Thinking my childhood friend was slow for not getting my meaning in the passage I mailed to her was the same attitude I took in my follow-up treatment program. By holding onto the delusions, the idea of mental illness couldn't be true. I couldn't believe I had bipolar.

And when I finally believed it, I got angry. If I had this thing called bipolar, I had it for years. Why the hell didn't someone see it earlier? If there was a better, more normal way to live, why didn't someone show me sooner? Why did I have to suffer such a catastrophe of a mental breakdown to realize some semblance of sanity?

As these thoughts compounded, I was near tears; with the journal on my lap feelings of helplessness came over me. I started to believe fairly convincingly that bipolar was true. I worried about what it meant for me and my future. I had to move past the denial of the condition now. I had to continue the journey toward acceptance and ultimately health. I had to grab hold of those around me to support me as I recovered. It had been months since I cracked. Early on, the doctors estimated the recovery would take six to eight weeks. I was not healthy yet, but I was better. I released the image of Jesus and saw the reality of my life with a mood disorder. Recovery hadn't been a straight line, but I surrendered to the process and it seemed to be working. In order to beat the beast, one must acknowledge the beast exists. In that moment, I gave up the weak belief that I wasn't a person living with bipolar. I knew I was, and I was ready to really apply the therapy that accompanied those constant doses of medication.

My husband woke up and found me on the couch with the journal and the markers looking like a child. Mike, who had always been respectful of my work in these journals, saw me with them and was about to leave me alone when I motioned him over.

"I found it," I said.

"What?" he said.

"Mania," I said. "Hypomania is there since my college days."

"Oh," he said.

I didn't show him the actual writing, because there was no need: he already knew mania was there, and he had been waiting, mostly patiently, for me to come to terms with the diagnosis. I was not emotional, but rather matter of fact when I revealed my discovery. He was kind to me as I shared this revelation to him. Of course, it was something he believed all along my path to wellness. He didn't press for more details; he didn't ask to read the passages I found. He only listened and then gently kissed me on the forehead before getting ready for work.

This piece of evidence kept me going to the doctors. I began bargaining with the disease I knew I had. Okay, I thought, I had bipolar, but that didn't mean I needed pills upon pills perpetually to treat it; I only needed to manage the symptoms. I thought again that I could toughen up enough to manage without medication someday. I thought the medications would be a temporary help that I could eventually wean from. I stopped arguing about meeting Jesus. I believed, however, I could make a deal with bipolar by vowing to recognize the symptoms, then make environmental adjustments to lessen bipolar's destruction.

After I found the first evidence of hypomania, strong memories came to me at random times bringing with them a punch of anxiety as I was reminded of other times in my life that were possibly classifiable as manic.

I once chased a man. Literally. I ran through a corn field to catch him harvesting corn, thinking he would be so happy to see me. He was combining corn in his fields in the dark, so I parked my car and ran through a muddy field to his tractor. I did this because I thought it was terribly romantic. Looking back, this humiliation also happened in a manic phase. We were reckless in our sexual relationship. The aftermath of this was an episode of major depression.

In 2006, another manic episode would have me practically walking out of the newspaper world — the best job fit I ever experienced — without a replacement job lined up. I had gotten angry one Thursday, because a goody-goody-corporate-type editor had called me at home. This seeming transgression infuriated me because I didn't think I made enough money to be so inconvenienced. I convinced Mike to let me quit the job. Because he thought I hated the job, he said we'd find a way to make our household budget work without me working there. On the following Monday, I walked into the managing editor's office with a paper signed with a two-week notice. He asked me what I wanted. I cried and said it wasn't in the building.

He had said, "Tara, if you ever figure out how good you are, you are going to be dangerous."

I had no idea what that meant. I still don't.

I have other memories of the humiliation of mania. When manic, I lose the ability to censor myself. I lose the ability to control my actions. When depressed, I lose the ability to act.

These storms of manic episodes explained a childhood of troublemaking; irrational decisions to leave jobs and lovers on a whim. And rage. God, forgive me for the rage and destruction. Each time a picture of mania came to me during recovery, I cringed as the truth of it hit me in the guts. I winced at the idea that it was really me who acted that way. I couldn't clearly remember mania before first finding it in a journal. I always rationalized the transgressions of those involved and denied my own inability to accurately see life. And when I knew I was wrong, I pushed those memories deep inside and vowed to do better. Every time I'd lose it, I'd scared myself and tried to move forward. I'd make apologies. Some forgave me; many didn't. Some people I've been able to reconcile with, others are simply left in my past. At the time, I thought I had bum luck. I didn't recognize all the good fortune I had all around me most of my life. I wasn't able to see and feel it, and I definitely couldn't hold onto it.

Health benefits exhausted

There was a cap: $10,000. That's the price my insurance company put on mental health treatment in a calendar year. Neither Mike nor I were aware of this cap until the bills started coming in the mail. It took about four months for the bills to work their way back out of insurance claim and back to medical providers and into our mailbox.

I was shocked when I checked the mail and saw these exuberant figures. A five-day, four-night stay at a psychiatric center costs more than a new car — a really nice new car. Meanwhile, bills from Lakeview Psychological Associates kept coming in. Up until the cap was reached, we had paid 10 percent of the cost; now we were responsible for 90 percent of the cost of each visit.

I couldn't look at the bills.

"How are we going to pay for this?" I asked Mike one day at the breakfast bar in our kitchen.

"Don't worry; I'll take care of it," Mike said.

But worry, I did. I felt guilty, responsible for having put my family through this ordeal. Not only had the experience been emotionally, socially, physically draining, but now I realized it was financially handicapping my family. I worried how we were going to absorb the costs. I worried about paying for celebrations for my three sons who all had birthdays coming that month. I worried about back-to-school fees, school supplies, and clothes for the older two boys.

I now resented the fact that I was off work while I recovered. I felt helpless. I had placed this entire burden on

Mike. He was steady. He said we would make arrangements to pay so much each month, evenly dividing what our budget could allocate to the various providers. This way, we'd slowly work the balance down.

I decided to do my part.

At my next visit with Dr. Carducci, I told her the problem.

"I can't afford to see you," I said, fully knowing the risk and cost of not seeing her.

I needed to find a way to health, so I could contribute to our family budget. But in the meantime, I had to reduce our medical expenses.

"Mike would be embarrassed to hear me say this, but we can't afford to pay our bill," I said. "We have to make payments."

"Most people can't afford psychological care," she said. "It's okay."

I daydreamed about her gifting her services, after having made enough money off me, but of course that couldn't happen. She had business expenses and needed to be compensated for her expertise. I didn't begrudge her rates, either; I believed she was worth what she charged. But I felt we were overextended, even though my family did everything right. I had worked, and Mike had a job with the city, which provided health insurance. This should have been enough to protect us from exuberant costs of medical care. And, to be fair, it was. We could make payments. We were not going to lose our house over it and we were not going to go hungry. We would make sacrifices. We wouldn't have a family vacation. The 10-year-old minivan wouldn't be replaced that year. Thomas would transfer to public school. The lifestyle we had worked so hard to build would be scaled back. Our savings would disappear. Our credit card balances would climb. Our luxuries would be removed. Yet, we would continue to work as hard as our peers, but go without eating out, new clothes, and updated household items.

A psychotic break, in my opinion, could not have been prevented. Through no real fault of my own and certainly no fault of Mike's or the kids', we were saddled with this expense. I felt tricked by the insurance company for selling me a false sense of security. The premiums were paid, yet the category of my health condition was exempt from coverage. This was allowed. Society thought this was okay. Society decided mental health doesn't count. As if it was in the category of braces or breast implants — or other luxuries — society has decided mental health treatment was optional.

Intellectually, I knew the cost of my care was not my fault. I knew I was a product of circumstance of a system that was broken. However, it was impossible to not feel responsible for the hardship. I felt, because my insurance company didn't recognize my health problem as anything physically wrong with me, but rather mental, it demoralized mentally ill patients, and by extension, classified me as weak and incapable of managing my mental health. I bought into this idea that I was weak, and thought, with enough gumption, I could have lived without treatment. Dr. Carducci, however, reminded me that I was sick and needed ongoing treatment. I was not well enough to be able to go back to work to afford treatment, yet I needed to regain health to be able to once again join of the ranks in productive society: it was a vicious cycle. She offered a compromised solution.

"What I can do is keep your appointments to 15 minutes, rather than 45," Dr. Carducci said. "You are getting better."

She also was willing to move my appointments to every other month, rather than every month. "Soon you will be well enough to only see me quarterly," she said.

I cried; I was embarrassed but grateful. She pulled the cardboard cube of tissues from the corner of her desk and gently set it on my lap. I pulled tissue after tissue as I tried to wipe and unclog my snot-filled nose. I gasped as I tried to regain composure. I came completely unglued. Shame from the condition and shame from the financial implications overwhelmed me. I kind of collapsed in defeat.

"Okay," I sighed.

"You have to call me if you get worse," she said. "And you have to call RIGHT AWAY if you develop a rash."

Since switching to Lamitical, we had been watching for a rash, which could indicate a side effect causing up to death. This risk subsided the longer I was on the medication.

"Okay," she said. "What I'm going to do is give you enough refills to last until I see you again. You have to promise to call me if anything gets worse."

As I left her tiny office, I noticed a child's colored picture taped to the door. Yet, I had not asked her about the picture. This was a professional, uneven relationship in which I told her everything about myself, and she revealed nothing of her personal life with me. It would have been a violation of etiquette to have inquired about the child in her life who had colored the picture. For months, while I had sat at the wall opposite the door and looked away from Dr. Carducci's face as I gathered my thoughts, I found my eyes settling on that picture. As she stood to open the door and release me to a hallway leading to the waiting room and reception area, the question about this coloring page was on the tip of my tongue. Yet again, I refrained. I simply walked out to see Jill at the desk. I made an appointment and Jill gave me a card with the time on it.

I walked back to my blue Dodge Grand Caravan and considered Dr. Carducci's comment that "most people can't afford their psychological care." It angered me.

If the insurance company didn't categorize my illness as anything other than mental why did I feel such physical pain? I knew the company was wrong. I felt it an incredible injustice. The cost of not treating mental illness exceeded the cost of treatment.

I started to feel some sort of personal responsibility to change this. I went home to Google NAMI, the National Alliance of Mental Illness, and see if there was some advocacy work that I could do. I didn't follow through. I was not strong enough, then.

In the meantime, I emailed my former contract supervisor to see about getting my job back.

Koi pond

I felt it was time to return to the two-day-a-week position as a grant manager handling transportation problems. I convinced my doctors to let me drive at high speeds. I talked to my supervisor and her supervisor, convincing them that I was stable enough to return to work. However, a condition of return was that I didn't send anymore emails to the county administrator about the yellow brick road (ugh, another pang of embarrassment that came from the manic episode which preceded the psychotic break). I had emailed him a disconnected list of solutions for the barriers preventing transportation coordination, using a metaphor comparing the work to Dorothy in "The Wizard of Oz." (The locals dub Ozaukee County the land of Oz; in fact there is a Wizard of Oz festival each year.) In my email, I had written about the yellow brick road and the way home. I remembered having felt so proud and bold and intelligent having solved the riddle of transportation coordination. I nodded with my head down and promised to refrain from emailing him.

My aunt Carol volunteered to come to my house two days a week and watch the little guys, who were both out of school for the summer. I had worked for four years in part-time, one-year grant management contracts, trying to implement programs that improve the life of those at risk. In 2007, I worked on fall prevention programming for the elderly. Since 2008, I worked on coordinating transportation for the elderly and people with disabilities under the title Mobility Manager.

Now, I was placed at the Aging and Disability Resource Center in Ozaukee County.

The gist of getting a mobility management program running was to identify the needs for transportation services and recognize the resources available. With this data, it was my job to connect the need with the service, identify gaps in service, and develop programs to meet those unmet needs. I learned techniques and approaches at national training events in Washington, D.C., in 2008 and Omaha, Nebraska, in 2009. I met inspirational people and learned strategies. I was good at what I did. Since my leave of absence, which lasted more than four months, program development had come to a halt. I had not been replaced, and with just five months left of the year, there was little to do. But with incredible kindness, my contract manager and her boss agreed to bring me back. My doctors released me back to work and removed the driving restriction. I took the freeway 50 miles to get to the office.

Located on an inside corridor without any windows, my office was along the hallway to the lunch room. People walked by often throughout the day to grab a yogurt, cup of coffee, or diet soda. It seemed every office that I ever worked in had a group of dieters who stocked the lunch room freezer with Lean Cuisines. Here was no exception; everyone talked about their Weight Watchers points and shared reduced-fat recipes and Cooking Light magazines. On the days I worked, I headed out to the nearest McDonald's or Culver's and drove to the lakeside park to eat my grease-laden lunch in my van alone.

It was weird being back to work. I had an office that I didn't get around to personalizing the first three months of the year. Michelle, my supervisor, told me one condition of returning to work was I had to cheer up the barren white walls. It was a half joke, but one to be taken seriously.

191

My office had a large desk, which was always clean. I had no caseload or projects underway. The walls were white. Many of the women who worked there — there were no men — were very creative and had beautifully decorated offices displaying their personalities. My walls remained void. I was intimidated as to what to reveal about my personality through decorating, and I had had no idea who I was or what I liked.

I settled on a red and orange print of two koi fish swimming the perimeter of a pond. Koi fish will only grow to the size that is sustainable to the size of its pond. Move the fish to a bigger pond and they grow. Keep them in a smaller pond and they remain the same size. There was no right size koi. They just adapted to their surroundings. The small fish seem trapped by circumstance in the print as they circled the edge with no place to grow. When I looked at it, I was tempted to metaphorically dream of a larger place for me. I reminded myself to not allow circumstance to confine me, but rather seek out places to grow. However, as people noticed my framed picture and asked about the fish. I just said, "I think they are pretty. I'd like a koi pond someday."

Basically, my work day consisted of sitting at an empty desk. The 8 1/2 hours went by slowly, but I tried to fill it as best I could. I started each morning with a to-do list, struggling to find tasks to fill it. I was basically an expert waiting for questions about the transportation services. I had to track the calls I got and log the solutions that were reached. I had to fill out grant reports. I got few emails and phone calls. I worked on coordinating a driver training class to help older adults retain their licenses and to educate them on the options available to them when the time came that they had to give up the keys. I filled out time cards and mileage reports, and registered for training, but that was about it. I limited my cigarette breaks to 10:30, 12:15 (combined with lunch), 2:45, and 4:15. I tried to avoid

Facebook, knowing they monitored my internet usage. I brought a jump drive and did some creative writing while waiting for the phone to ring. I gulped down the guilt and appreciated this bit of circumstance in which I was a beneficiary.

Loony Bin

"Hello?"

"Hello Paul, this is Tara. I'm in the loony bin."

"Huh?" he said.

"Hello Paul, this is Tara. I'm in the loony bin," I repeated.

"Patty, it's for you," he told his wife, my aunt.

I didn't remember this conversation happening, but there was a lot I didn't remember.

I heard the story when it was told at the family gathering about five months after I was released from the psychiatric center. I laughed with the rest of the family as it surfaced. I asked for the dictation of the conversation to be retold over and over to accurately store it to memory. I wanted to be certain I captured the exact words to unravel the mystery of my mental illness. Like a chef who tasted the same dish again and again trying to pull out the flavors that blended into something complete, I spent my time since release pulling memories of my own and those around me to try to figure out the recipe for clinical insanity.

On Labor Day, the extended family gathered together for a fish fry of Grandpa Jim's Michigan-caught pan fish: bluegills, crappies and a few perch. As the story of a phone call to my aunt Patty was shared, I laughed — not because it was funny, but because it was ludicrous. It was ludicrous because I didn't belong in a loony bin, and absurd because I was so deadpan in my conversation. Laughter, in this regard, served as a release from something uncomfortable, something we all knew was true. I laughed at the ridiculousness of having told my uncle I was in a loony bin, because I wanted to believe, just a little bit, the experience was as trivial as suggested by the words "loony" and "bin." I wanted to poke fun at the few screws that were loosened. I wanted to appreciate the joke and laugh at it. This fit of laughter had tears escaping from my eyes. But each time the story was retold, I laughed a little less as I processed the conversation's significance. And I noticed Mike wasn't laughing at all.

I was the one who had brought up the subject of my hospitalization and subsequent bipolar diagnosis with my mother's youngest sister, Patty, who was just eleven years my senior. She had been a friend and confidant throughout my life. When I was young, Patty babysat for me. Later, she selected me as godmother for her only child, because, as she put it then, I needed something positive in my life. Patty owned a vitamin store and was holistic in her approach to a healthy life; she ate organic foods, and she had done so long before it became vogue. Patty wore shoes with a slight heel. She shopped in the juniors department, but always managed to look sophisticated despite her tiny frame.

I had asked Patty if she knew I had been hospitalized in the spring. I felt it was an obvious secret in the room that no one wanted to initiate discussing. This was the first time since Easter we had all gotten together. The conversations to this point were as innocent as back to school, growing children, and the weather: it was a party after all. However, there was mention of some things a bit more serious. We discussed Cousin Molly's new job. We took up Uncle Jim's surgeries and physical medical problems. We talked about Mom blowing out her knee, but no one had broached the subject of my insanity. No one asked me how I had been feeling or how treatment was going. It was as if — even in the company of my family — the subject of mental illness remained taboo.

This subject was off limits until I grew restless enough to demand its attention. My family wanted to assume that although something had happened to me, I was better now and it was best to just forget and keep quiet. The episode of psychosis, the subsequent inpatient therapy, and then later home-based treatment was something to lock away in the closet of family secrets. Tucked away, so the embarrassment of the incident could be forgotten like the time someone had too much to drink at cousin so and so's wedding.

Patty confessed she knew of my hospitalization and said, "You called me. You don't remember that. I was crying when I got off the phone."

Her husband Paul then lightened the mood by revealing the phone call I made from the hospital. Paul married into the family in the mid-1990s. He generally spent his time at gatherings reading the newspaper and observing the interactions of the rest of the family members.

The exact dialogue of the conversation I had after Paul handed Patty the phone wasn't retold at the fish fry. After the comical portion Paul had shared, the rest was too painful to even pull off a slice of hilarity. Once Patty took the phone, I had accused her of contributing to my mental breakdown because she had provided supplements the month before the incident to aid my whacked thyroid.

While hospitalized, the doctors asked me about drug usage; I determined the vitamins were drugs and attributed their use to Patty's pure intentions of helping me find health. Sequestered in the confines of the locked hospital wing, I looked for someone to blame, and later I was sorry to discover that I misdirected it in her direction. The jury was still out on what caused bipolar and psychosis, but I was growing past anger and assigning blame in order to accept the diagnosis as a condition of my whole.

It wasn't until Patty reminded me of my phone call to her that it was reinstated to memory. I didn't fully remember calling her or anyone else from the confines of the facility. It astonished me that I had access to a phone and the freedom to use it. I also was amazed I had recollected a phone number I never enter into my key pad, because it was programmed into my cell phone. Did I call her from my cell phone? Did someone give me her number so I could call her from a hospital phone? Did I dial "9" to reach an outside line? Did I have the cognition to do these things?

At the gathering, my mother admitted she jotted Patty's number for me on a piece of paper when she visited me. I wondered who else, if anyone, came to see me. I knew my husband Mike was there. He had told me he watched me sleep, before being shooed out of my patient room in a violation of protocol, and had left behind the leather case with a journal inside as a get-well gift. I remembered seeing Mike and my oldest son Joseph on a day when I was awake and walking around.

I thought I remembered clearly all that had happened from the five days of hospitalization, and I was humbled to discover chunks of events that never made it to my memory. My aunt Patty believed the medications I was given at the hospital to bring me down from the psychosis had caused this selective amnesia. I made a mental note to request my medical records to determine what these medications were.

As I collected clues to the mystery of the missing moments from my memory, Mom told me there was a phone in my room. My cousin, Molly, admitted I left a voicemail message for her telling her I was locked away, but that she didn't call me back. I waited for the "me too" of phone calls I had made from the hospital, but I only get a "hey what about me?" response from my friend Catherine.

After Paul's story, I thought I'd found an opening in the conversation in which to share my experience. I tried to tell my family about the breakdown and what it is like to live with the new bipolar diagnosis, but I couldn't get an audience who wanted to listen to the horrors of psychosis. It was as if they thought my talking about it would make it contagious or more kindly take me back into its grasp. My family didn't want to hear it. So I had to let the conversation end.

"It just comes down to stress," my uncle Tony said.

Tony was a straight shooter, who hunted and fished and drove a pick-up truck. He seemed far too tough and steady to accept something as flighty as mental illness as real.

"Some days I think I have ADD," Patty said. "Seriously, I am always forgetting and losing things."

She didn't know it wasn't called that anymore. Attention Deficit Disorder was by then classified as ADHD (Attention Deficit Hyperactivity Disorder). It was broken into two categories: impulsivity type and inattentive type. But she simply didn't know.

The mainstream media published a string of symptoms that are common in a mental disorder, leading people to the conclusion that they had the condition. What they failed to realize is that these forms of mental illness also had to disrupt daily life.

Molly told me about having panic attacks and anxiety problems, which she overcame with prayer.

No one, of course, said they were bipolar, or manic depressive as it was formerly called. No one confessed to this disease. They categorized my psychotic break and subsequent diagnosis as some sort of extension of the run-of-the-mill-ups-and-downs-of-so-called-normal life. They wanted to connect with me, so they shared their own stories. I couldn't imagine they meant any disrespect. They couldn't possibly understand what it was like to have been stripped to such a

198

state of nothingness and then to walk toward health, only to find people giving what they thought was advice and encouragement, but really only served to rear mental illness's steadfast companion — denial. Denial of the disease snuck back in, just when I thought I was getting closer to acceptance.

My family did not realize comparing a nervous breakdown to a mild case of anxiety or forgetfulness is like telling a person with skin cancer that they once had sunburn and little bit of aloe gave relief.

"Have you tried the aloe?"

How absurd. No one would suggest such a treatment for skin cancer. Yet, as I recovered from my breakdown, it was often regarded as something other than a serious medical problem. The advice I often encountered was to exercise, modify my diet, take some supplements, or try meditation or prayer. It was implied that I should forgo the science and chemical treatments offered by psychiatry. And a good laugh with a cold beer or warm glass of merlot would do me some good as well.

While my family hosted a confession session of ailments and offered some remedies that I should maybe try, I left my parents' kitchen and stepped to the patio. Once again, denial of bipolar disorder's truth snuck into my thoughts. I knew if I stayed with the family, I would again believe I was weak and that a stronger person could muster the courage to forgo treatment and dismiss the reality of bipolar as a legitimate disorder. I thought I had already worked through denial and had accepted the mental illness. However, the idea that the psychosis was a fluke and my bipolar diagnosis was a mistake was a possibility I continued to wrestle with.

I lit up a cigarette. My sister Billie joined me outside, though she didn't smoke. Again the tears came, but not like the release of joy that came during the loony bin's laughter fit.

The tears this time escaped as I questioned if these well-meaning family members were correct. Did I just need to be mentally tough and get over myself and this diagnosis of bipolar? Couldn't I just chalk it up to the ups and downs of normal life?

Billie assured me I was not crazy to believe in mental illness. As a teacher in a public school, her classroom was filled with ED high school students (ED stands for Emotionally Disturbed). Billie held a master's degree in special education. I trusted her opinion; she told me that she could recognize the disease as part of my life since childhood. As Billie assured me I should stick with the treatment program, she reminded me about the advances in science that are finding more evidence of mental illness as a bona fide sickness such as the brain imaging that lit up abnormalities. That gave me hope.

I started to explain my frustration with the people who assumed I just had a case of stress mismanagement, but I stopped, because really, what was the point in finding fault in the beliefs of my family members and in the larger scope the mainstream? They were not to blame for the misunderstanding of mental illness.

At the fish fry, I was ready to tell my story of mental illness, but my family wasn't ready to hear the truth; they may never be. Besides, it wasn't the right venue for such a tale. In fact, there really wasn't a social setting appropriate for sharing the story of mental illness.

I decided to keep my conversations to the weather, the delight of my growing children, or the satisfaction I got from writing. My own health was a subject I decided to keep to myself, because it was best to keep social banter light and positive. Mental illness, in my mind, was lumped into the other off-color subjects of polite conversation such as sex, religion, and politics.

I learned not to express the reality of my mental illness in my public life, too. I used euphemisms. I disrespected the disease. I pooh-poohed it. I laughed at it. I denied its seriousness. I wanted to go on as if I didn't have bipolar, so I made jokes about it. I trivialized it. I found a way to make it funny and therefore acceptable. I simply blended in with the rest of the world and kept my diagnosis a secret that everybody knew, but nobody talked about.

My experience, when I told people I had bipolar, was they didn't believe me anyway. The exceptions were only those people who happen to know intimately someone afflicted with the disorder. Sometimes I felt the need to convince the world that mental illness was real, but really I only needed to confidently and completely accept it as real for me.

"Everyone's dealing with something," Uncle Tony said.

And Tony was right.

For civility's sake, I concurred the tales of mental illness remained taboo. But my bipolar and its manic episode that crossed into psychosis was a story I couldn't keep to myself. I needed to understand its horrific detail, to reach clarity, and to reveal its truth. I remembered strings of imperfect memories and pulled them like taffy until those memories became lost in their individuality. It was my hope the entanglement of tales could be woven into a tapestry of acceptance.

PART FOUR: EVER AFTER

October 2010 – March 2011

PTSD

The conference center's dining room was empty, except for Mark sitting alone at a table set for five. Mark had a strong, no-nonsense, one-syllable name and exuded the type of confidence demanding respect and a little piece of fear.

We were attending a three-day work training session, the fourth in a series of five annual meetings designed to train us in our work as mobility managers. With my illness, I missed the spring and summer sessions. That fall I returned to a group where I was once respected as a leader. The previous morning, I sat alone for breakfast while groups of colleagues sat in small groups creating a buzz of camaraderie. I woke earlier that morning, hoping to avoid my public display of loneliness, hoping to have the restaurant to myself. But there sat Mark, a man who I had seen at several training sessions and work conferences over the past few years but hardly knew. Holding a paper cup of coffee in my hand, I walked over to the former Chicago cop who was less intimidating seated than when he stood (at six feet tall, with broad shoulders and thick thighs, his physique was hard to overlook).

"Can I join you … or are you waiting for your friends?" I asked.

With his mouth full of food, he gestured for me to sit in an empty seat. Leaving a chair between us on one side and two empty chairs separating us on his other side, I sat not quite directly across from him.

"How are you doing?" he asked.

"Mental breakdowns aren't for sissies," I said, hinting at my own toughness to muster through the illness and my courage to return to a place where I once not only belonged but also had been respected by my peers. During the past couple of days, group interactions had told me that respect was gone, yet they had granted me access to return. Against the advice of my physicians, I had announced the embarrassing sickness not just to my boss, but also to the entire association in an email — an act I regretted as I walked among colleagues who avoided me, apparently afraid I would crack, or maybe just afraid I was contagious. On top of the feeling of not belonging, I was not sure what I was doing there. I knew I would not, could not continue in the field of transportation coordination, at least not in Wisconsin, where the members of this professional association had avoided eye contact with me. I was clearly no longer one of them. I was clearly less than I was six months ago. I was certain that had I had broken limbs that caused my medical leave, I would not have been so ostracized.

"Oh, I know," Mark said. "I have been going through my own mental shit."

Stuck in my head surrounded by embarrassment for having returned to place as "that girl with mental issues," I was surprised by the confession of this solid, confident man.

We were interrupted by a waitress. Because I wanted to hear Mark's story of his own "mental shit," I recited my order before being asked for it: "Two eggs over hard, hash browns, and whole wheat toast."

She dutifully wrote down my order and then shared a story with us about it being the busy season at the indoor water park/resort/conference center. As we feigned interest and asked her additional questions, I mentally processed what Mark had said, wondering what kind of "mental shit" he could possibly be going through. Since being sick, I felt so isolated, alone, and weak. Admittedly, since it was my first experience with severe mental shit, I was certain no one else could have possibly experienced something similar. I had grown protective of my experience and believed no one else could possibly understand. At least not in a real way that touched on the severity of what had happened to me.

After the waitress left, Mark shared his story.

"I have been struggling with what they call PTSD," he said.

"It wasn't always like this. For years, I was fine. I don't know, you get older and you start to think about ..." Mark paused, collecting his thoughts.

I nodded.

"For years, I was fine. Nothing bothered me. I didn't think about it," he said. "Then I went to this VA doctor, told him I was having trouble sleeping. That fucker. Sorry."

"It's okay. Go on," I said.

"Well, he said I should let it out, I should remember it. I wish I never would have seen him. Now. Well, now, I can't get it to stop."

"I have nightmares with bright red blood pouring from bodies. The image of the blood is so vivid. It's bright red. I can't shake the picture. I wake up and I can still see it, smell it. The pictures are on a steady loop that keeps reeling."

"You have to understand. I was in charge. Guys in my group were being killed. It was kill or be killed, and I wasn't going to watch any more of my guys get killed."

The waitress came back to bring my food. Soon after, she returned to check on us, but everything was fine with our meals. She left quickly. Still, no one entered the dining room.

I thought about what his story meant. The nightmares were the replaying of real bloodshed: foreign men killed by his doing and by those he commanded to do the same. The advice of the VA doctor to bring these memories to the surface bubbled up the horrific realization, and recognition, of what had happened. Mark remembered images that no one should ever have had witnessed or participated in: Memories of a war disrespected, memories of a time no one wanted to hear about. He couldn't get the memories to stop.

He explained how he had seen too many of his soldiers killed at enemy hands. He had gone on a government-supported mission, which never had the backing of the people, to kill those whom he referred to as "gooks."

He apologized again, this time for using the language. He knew it was wrong by today's standards. I winced when he used the word, just a little bit, but I understood it. Years of hosting sensitivity training workshops had conditioned me to avoid using derogatory stereotypes, but one culture appreciation class in college taught me to understand where this type of slang came from. By classifying the enemy soldiers as gooks, it dehumanized them. A person could rationalize killing a gook, but when he stopped to think he was really killing a soldier, a man, the emotions tripped up the mission, the goal. To stay alive, the soldiers had to make someone else die. It was that simple. Young men on both sides (I imagined mirror images of boys dressed in opposing uniforms) were executed. Mark was haunted by these facts. And to this day, he couldn't admit out loud these were men. He had to kill the gooks, the people who were less than people.

I listened to his story. He was desperate to make the nightmares, which left him in cold sweats, end. I had no knowledge base to help him, no advice to give. As we finished our meals and settled our bills, we looked at one another, a silent glance of solidarity. Mental illness was a cross to bear alone. It was not respected. It was embarrassing, a mark of inability to handle stress.

Our solemn glance said, "It's okay. I understand."

His friends started to shuffle into the dining room then, their bodies heavy and groggy from the lounge drinking that took place the night before. I stood and left the table, making room for the guys to join their friend, as I excused myself to pack. Mark stayed. I heard him laugh with his friends as the shenanigans of the previous evening were recounted. I was, for the first time, grateful for my disease and having the courage to stand up and simply tell the world I suffered from mental illness. This bold (and really it was more naiveté than courage) sharing of my experience and its truth compelled Mark to tell me another truth. With conversations, understanding and respect could come. Compassion could follow. I wondered what got us both up so early that day. I entertained the notion a higher power arranged for us to talk while, at the same time, acknowledged a mere coincidence had occurred. Quite possibly, Mark was woken early by a nightmare. I didn't know if Mark needed to tell his story or I needed to hear it. Either way, my stupidity of announcing a psychotic break in a mass email allowed two people to break bread together and remind ourselves that humanity takes many forms. None of us was really as okay as the face we presented. And all of us were okay enough to heal and continue to take our places in life.

I saw a glimpse of humanity over breakfast. I saw a story of a veteran. The term Post Traumatic Stress Disorder had a face. With a face, it became real. We afflicted with mental illness hid this face in our day-to-day encounters. We did not display the mental suffering. We kept the wounds, the injuries, the healing scabs, and scars concealed. We were tough. We were strong. The world would have looked at us and thought we were pathetic for admitting mental illness, which could be perceived as weakness. That morning, I tried to take it easy on myself and just a little bit rewrite the vocabulary in my mind. I did not "admit" I had a mental illness in that email. Rather, I revealed a truth of the human condition. I showed that even respected and successful people are not immune to insanity. I realized, to most, changing that word will not make its way to common vernacular. The world will still look at those who say they are bipolar or have PTSD as guilty of something that they should probably keep to themselves rather than admit that they are crazy.

They Saw

The best working diagnosis was still "some form of bipolar." Everyone working for the past nine months was under the impression that I had untreated bipolar disorder, beginning with the first depression — postpartum following my oldest son's birth. It is a misunderstanding to consider the disease omnipresent; I found it helpful to accept that the disease flared up at different times of my life. According to the Diagnostic and Statistical Manual of Mental Disorders (DSM-IV), a person only needs to experience one episode of mania or hypomania to be considered bipolar rather than having a unipolar disorder, namely depression.

I wanted to shrug away denial for good and just get on with living with a disease that I could manage. I wrestled with the idea that I could be both healthy and sane while also accepting the bipolar disorder. I wanted an understanding of what it would take to reach this final step of recovery. Ironically, once I had started considering myself a woman living with a feared mental illness, I began to act more sane and rational. I committed to the program set forth by my doctors early on in fear of returning to the psychosis that I experienced that necessitated admission to the psychiatric care unit. I had stepped through denial, anger, and bargaining; I finally was close to allowing the disease to be part of my human condition. I also accepted that there was no cure, only treatment; I resolved to take mood stabilizers for the rest of my life. Life had become so much more pleasant with the help of the medications and the fear of losing my family or hurting myself or others trumped that appeal to simply toughen up.

The medical community was able to place my psychotic break into the context of my long history of depression and conclude I had a bipolar mood disorder right away. When I looked back at life through the diagnosis' reflective lens, a lot of pain and destruction was explainable although not excusable. I, the person — not the disease personified — acted out the destruction. I decided the more interesting part of my story and journey was not internal at all; a self-examined life can only take one so far. To really understand what happened to me, I needed to see the perspectives of my care team and support system. I put this off for so long, because, in part, I knew throughout recovery that my mental illness diagnosis was accurate. The diagnosis rang true and was at once a relief and a defeat. But I was not ready to be defeated. During that year, I began to understand how the disease could hurt me but not entirely destroy me. I only needed to recognize the limitations it presented and rely on medication to negate the effects of the disease on my person.

To better understand what I looked like from the outside in, I requested my medical records from the psychiatric health center. They arrived in the mail about a week later. I saw the envelope but was afraid to open it right away. I set it on the oak dining room table. I quieted the children. I set Alex up to watch an episode of *Word World*, recorded from PBS morning cartoons. Thomas played a lap-held, age-appropriate Fisher-Price computer game.

This allowed me about twenty minutes of uninterrupted time. I opened the 10# regular envelope and found a thick stack of stapled documents. I gazed over them, reading quickly. Then I poured over them, reading intently. Some words I understood, but many more were jargon and medical and their definitions escaped me.

212

Immediately, it became obvious that what I experienced and what the world saw were two entirely different things. Likely, the more interesting and relevant thing was what they saw.

The records started out harmless enough as they described the intake assessment, "Tara is a 33-year-old, married female who lives with her husband, 11-year-old son, and two children ages 2 and 4. She has been working as a mobility manager for the Department of Aging Resources through Ozaukee County."

These records said I was referred to the closest inpatient facility from the Holy Family EAP (Employee Assistance Program) Department located in my hometown presenting, according to my husband, "an acute onset of agitation, inability to sleep, and hallucinations."

The paperwork was broken into categories that someone had completed in a neat computer-generated form. Under the "History of Present Illness" section it read,

> "Tara apparently has a previous history of 'cyclothymia' and possible attention deficit hyperactivity disorder. She had seen a Dr. Daniel Burbach, a psychologist at Lakeview Clinic in Manitowoc, about a year ago. She had been maintaining on Wellbutrin XL 150 mg in the morning."

I wondered where this information came from. No one ever had used the term "cyclothymia" with me. And the ADHD was a self-diagnosed excuse to take Joseph's Focalin from time to time.

The assessment of me at intake began quickly on the first page:

> "The patient presents today to our intake department as being 'floridly' psychotic. She was

disoriented, unable to cooperate, and wandering through the lobby kissing and hugging people. Her mood ranged from euphoric to angry and she initially refused medication in treatment."

I didn't know what floridly meant, and I had no memory of hugging and kissing people in the lobby. As I read the scene described, however, I recollected a memory of the hospital lobby. A nurse was walking a black middle-sized dog with long hair on a leash down the hallway. I was not a dog person, but I was overcome with the beauty of the animal in that moment. I left Mike's side and got on my hands and knees to crawl to the dog while I made noises trying to get the dog to come to me. When the dog and I met, I hugged and petted him. Then I kissed him. After reading the medical documents, I wondered if there was a dog at all. Was it really a person that I hugged and kissed?

I didn't remember anyone offering medication to me. In short, I wasn't at the same place as these records were indicating. That was somewhere else; I was somewhere trapped in my subconscious makings.

According to the file, Mike had told the staff I had been, "a bit more energetic the past week." He also told them I had been "preoccupied and frustrated with (my) job with Ozaukee County, actually 'challenging them to fire her' because she feels that she is not given enough responsibility in her position."

The medical records continued,

"during the past few days, (I) began 'talking crazy' ... (I) started to feel that Ozaukee County should 'bring me their problems and I will solve them' ... She also believes that if she is able to quit her job she will become a 'poet laureate.' She also has been preoccupied with her husband attending Catholic

Church saying that he should come to convert with her."

I remembered being consumed with the idea of a higher calling to do something extraordinary in my life. The poetry I wrote was never published, and I lacked any formal training in the craft. Yet I remembered thinking I should be a poet laureate, and even discussed the idea with my boss of having Ozaukee County hiring me as a full-time poet. A poet, in my mind, was the person wise enough to solve any problem with lyrics that could creatively spark solutions. This had made complete and total sense to me at the time. What a racket! As I read it printed in front of me, I saw how loony I was and why the word crazy was used in common vernacular. I didn't read as ill or sick. It read as something else — a personality flaw or behavior shortcoming.

The records talked about my preoccupation with Joseph's wrestling tournament in the weeks leading up to the break. The state youth wrestling tournament in Madison began on a Friday night and I was committed the following Monday afternoon. According to the records, when Mike arrived Saturday in Madison, "he noticed that (I) was much more agitated, disorganized and not sleeping. (I) reported that (I have) been hearing the voices of the husband's mother and sister, the voice of Martin Luther King, and the voices of various boys on the wrestling team."

I didn't remember any of this. I read the information and denied it was true. But there it was in black and white, proof what the world saw of me.

Blessedly, my husband completely denied any prior similar episodes. However, somehow the intake department did "notice that the patient has a history of 'cutting off all of her hair about a year ago.'" I remembered the frustration I had had with my appearance during a depressed phase. I took a scissors to my head, started with the bangs, and before I left the mirror had chopped my shoulder-length hair into a terrible pixie cut. I didn't remember sharing this with the intake staff. In fact, I didn't remember talking with anyone that day I was committed. It amazed me how much personal information was garnered without having had my conscious understanding or consent.

Mike didn't hold back when he told the staff,

"(I) also (have) a history of being aggressive, yelling at spouse, and reportedly throwing things and breaking them. When (my) moods change, (I) can become destructive, he states. He feels that (my) moods in particular change before (my) menstrual cycle and (I) did have an episode of postpartum depression after the birth of one of (our) sons."

The report included a "Past Psychiatric History," which revealed I had no prior hospitalizations, had seen Dr. Burbach at Lakeview Psychiatric, and that I "self-diagnosed myself with ADHD," and Mike suspected I was "getting into some of my son's Focalin."

In the family history portion, Mike reported no other mental illness in my family of origin but did describe my family as "colorful people."

Mike described my alcohol and drug history as just very minimal alcohol use. He apparently told the staff that I did drink over the weekend in Madison but not to any great extent. The report included my current medication and notes that I have been "training for a 10K run" without any prior history of being a runner.

Perhaps the most disturbing was the picture of my personal and development history. I didn't remember sharing this information with them, so the information was gathered without my knowledge. I had vacated my mind, and those left behind were intrusive enough to paint the picture of me they could see.

> "Tara was born in the Reedsville area. She has no known history of abuse or neglect. She did attend two years of college and recently she has been getting her undergraduate degree at the University of Wisconsin-Green Bay. Her degree is going to be 'interdisciplinary' and it frustrates her that her degree is not more specific, according to her spouse. She previously worked as a writer for the Manitowoc newspaper. Her husband describes her as a very gifted author. She apparently is quite frustrated with her job. Her religious affiliation is Roman Catholic. Her husband is involved in the city services in Manitowoc."

They listed my strengths as "intelligent" and "a good writer." Another strength listed was "good resources for treatment," which I assumed meant I had health insurance and a savings account.

In the portion of the report called "Mental Status Examination," the meat of the problem was transcribed, and it was a scary image:

> "Tara is presenting as a disheveled, loud, incoherent female who is agitated and uncooperative in the intake department. She is not making any sense. Her speech is disorganized. She was refusing medication. As noted above, she was wandering around the hospital entrance hugging and kissing people. She has no apparent thoughts of suicide and no history of suicidal or homicidal ideation or behaviors. She does have grandiose delusions that she is going to be 'a poet laureate.' She may be vaguely paranoid. She feels that her employers are under-utilizing her.

She has some religious preoccupation in terms of her husband converting to Catholicism. According to her husband, she has been fairly agitated about that. She has been reporting that she is hearing the voices of her husband's mother and sister. She hears the voices of Martin Luther King and the wrestling team. The husband is not aware of what the voices are saying. She has no apparent visual hallucinations."

The medical assessment done by professionals said, "The patient is disoriented to date and time. She is aware that she is at a psychiatric facility, but she is not able to state which facility." This was inconsistent with my memory as well. I didn't remember anyone asking me where I was, and I certainly didn't know I was being admitted to the ICU unit of the psychiatric hospital.

"She is unable to cooperate with memory testing. She cannot repeat three words due to her level of agitations," the report continued. "She cannot complete calculations. She cannot count backward from 10 due to agitation."

The initial diagnostic impressions were defined in five segments:

•Axis I - Psychotic disorder, not otherwise specified, acute onset with histories of a mood disorder, not otherwise specified, premenstrual Dysphoric disorder, and postpartum depression;

•Axis II – Diagnosis deferred;

•Axis III – History of hypothyroidism;

•Axis IV: Psychosocial and environmental problems are moderate to severe — working 20 hours a week, graduating from college, three young children.

•Axis V: Global assessment of functioning on admission 15, highest level in the past year unspecified.

I had no idea what any of that meant. When I saw my doctors, they didn't tell me how they categorized the problem; they didn't explain to me what they were thinking. They only asked me more of what I was thinking, feeling, doing.

I couldn't process the medical procedures, so I flipped the page to the discharge summary to see what they were saying about me when I left the facility. Physically, which I assumed to mean non-mental health, they apparently did a check-up-type exam and found I had hypothyroidism and history of asthma. The recommendation was to draw blood to check thyroid level. Also, because of a history of anemia they needed to check CBC. Again, I wondered how this information and the consent of this probe were attained.

The records described my experience at the hospital through the point of view of the medical staff:

"Tara was admitted in a severely agitated state, throwing food, biting staff, requiring IM medication. She calmed with a combination of Geodon IM 20 mg, which was administered twice and Lorazepam combination of up to 3 mg. Because of her positive response to Geodon, (the doctor) initiated routine Geodon dosing of 40 mg p.o. at q.a.m. and 80 mg p.o. with supper. Lorazepam was also initiated at a dosage of 0.5 mg p.o t.i.d. and 1 mg p.o. at bedtime. She continued to have sleep problems and therefore a second dose of Geodon was initiated to 100 mg and Geodon increased to 40 mg q.a.m. and q. noon. Lorazepam was advanced to 2 mg and Benadryl 50 mg added at h.s. to avoid an extrapyramidal symptom reaction."

"Tara gradually cleared over her few days in the hospital. She continued to go in and out of episodes of confusion and mild grandiosity, talking about subjects such as "coliseums" and comparing her husband to a "a duck, not a yacht." She declined to talk to (the doctor) on the first day, on the second day she began asking about her condition and by the date of discharge she seemed to be more clear and coherent in terms of describing the triggers for this hospitalization being the stress of juggling school, work, and parenting."

The next part of the record revealed the assessment of my mental status on the date of discharge, April 2, where a "family meeting" was held with the doctor, Mike, and my mom. While I didn't remember any of this conversation the way it was recorded, I read that my family (and I) alluded to a long-standing history of mood cycling with episodes of hypomania, decreased need for sleep, an increase in activity, rapid speech, and a tendency to take on too many projects. Unfortunately, these episodes tended to be followed by episodes of depression. It was noted that per history I had temporarily responded to a number of antidepressants but then became "immune to them."

The question was raised as to whether or not I had been using my son's Focalin prior to this admission. I admitted at one point that I had in fact been using it, later I said perhaps only "once a month." It was explained that the combined use of antidepressant and Focalin in a patient who might be vulnerable to bipolar might have brought out this type of reaction and, combined with a lack of sleep, the patient experienced a brief psychotic episode as a result.

They typed out an assessment of my mental status on discharge, which stated I complained of sleepiness during the mid morning but was basically fairly awake and alert in the late afternoon. I was noted as having some difficulty with concentration and, at times, some thought disorganization. Nurses described my mood as continuing to be somewhat "labile." They said I might go for an hour being fairly calm and coherent, then for five or ten minutes I might be a bit more agitated, anxious and perhaps intrusive. I apparently continued to request discharge repeatedly. They noted I did not appear to be actively delusional at the time of discharge, and I denied any suicidal or homicidal ideation during this admission. I also denied hearing voices before the admission, and I denied hallucinations at the time of discharge.

At the time of discharge, the doctor was recommending another one or two days in the hospital due to my ongoing mood labiality and periods of brief confusion. This came as a surprise to me; I recalled nothing of this suggestion. Thankfully, Mike and my mom agreed that because the Easter holiday was coming up, they would bring me home and supervise me over the weekend. Outpatient appointments were scheduled for the Monday after discharge back in Green Bay, in order to review my response to medications.

I read the prognosis section and was relieved to see it was good overall, and it mentioned that I have good insight and access to care. The final diagnosis from the inpatient experience was a psychotic disorder, not otherwise specified, suspected bipolar disorder mixed with psychotic features.

The record included information from my follow-up visit the following Monday:

"Tara is here with her husband after having been discharged from the adult inpatient unit three days ago. She actually seems to be doing very well. She has been socializing, attending a family picnic,

221

spending time with her family, going to church. She feels slowed down, somewhat over focused, and at times confused. She has difficulty tracking time. She will initiate an activity but forget what she had started. On a very positive note, she does not seem to be distraught, upset, nor manic. Her anxiety is under good control. She is sleeping well, she does not seem to be delusional nor is she experiencing hallucinations. Her husband sees things as being much improved."

The doctor considered me "surprisingly calm, agreeable, my insight is fairly good." She noted my speech was a bit slowed but linear and logical. Of course, she documented that I was not suicidal or homicidal. She also said I had no signs of a thought disorder or delusional thinking or hallucinations.

There was some tinkering with the medications to reduce the doses. And the records continued by noting my next outpatient appointment in my hometown.

Additionally, FMLA papers were completed for Mike and a letter was written to the University of Wisconsin-Green Bay asking to delay my deadlines and/or asking that I be allowed to drop classes. Regarding my employment questions, I was advised to defer any decisions for the next two months.

Some of this I knew, most of it I didn't. The severity of the situation was hammered in my mind after reading the records: I could no longer consider the novelty of the journey.

Mike's Love

I bid a final farewell to the idea that I met Jesus without fanfare. I quietly accepted that the insights I garnered while psychotic were nothing more than rubbish.

As part of putting together the pieces as to what led me to psychosis, Mike had taken the scribbling I created on Palm Sunday to the doctor in Green Bay. He was trying to find a way to explain what characterized my behavior in the time leading up to hospitalization. These dot-matrix paper rolls recorded what I believed then as the Word of God.

They were not saved as part of my medical file. They were discarded like one recycles their child's 100th finger painting. This wisdom that demanded transcription was no more masterful than a drunk's. I didn't reach any epiphanies. The doctors must have seen what they consider illustrations of clanging and, having seen it before countless times, recorded its existence and discarded it.

"It is as if you thought you were a prophet," my mother said to me once over the summer.

She came close. I didn't think I was a prophet, I knew I was the chosen one. The knowledge I gleaned that night at the cusp of insanity was still real in my mind. I considered the psychosis as almost a romanticized out-of-body experience. Even as I grew better and healthier, I still thought there was a chance that I was selected for a special message. My hold on this belief loosened as the medication and support system worked to remove me from the crippling grasp of this symptom of mental illness. Receiving the medical records sealed my fate as ordinary.

I had wanted to decipher the work coded in the pictures and words drawn with colored pencils. But since there were not saved, I just had my imperfect memory of them. I remembered the word promise. I remembered the number five. I remembered working frantically. I couldn't remember what else was recorded. It was like I had colored on the bathroom mirror in lipstick, and the cleaning lady washed it clear before anyone could see or read it.

When I had opened that package from the mailman with my medical records, I knew there was a chance the pictures would be missing, but I looked nonetheless. I finally realized what Dr. Carducci said in May was true: "They probably just threw them away," she had said.

When I heard that, I looked to my right on the couch where Mike sat beside me. He shrugged, but I was livid. This was very personal work, and I felt immensely violated after learning the papers were picked up and shared as clues to my insanity. I was pissed off at Mike for giving my drawings from this time to the doctors — this felt like a huge betrayal to hand over my important work to others. I thought then there was a conspiracy against me. I didn't realize that episode of looking out the window was a symptom; I didn't realize the drawings at the table also were crazy.

Later, when Mike came home from work, I told him the medical records had been delivered with the day's mail and that the colored illustrations were not part of the package. There was no anger in my voice. I finally understood.

"What was it like? Really like?" I asked him.

"It was scary," he said.

"Was I really hugging and kissing people in the lobby?" I asked.

Mike nodded.

"Did I bite someone?"

"I'm not sure," he said.

"Was there a dog?" I asked.

"I don't think so," Mike said.

"How did you know what to do?"

"Tara, I knew something was seriously wrong," he said.

"How?" I asked.

"Tara, you peed on the dining room floor," he said.

"NO! No, I didn't. Really?" I said, knowing at this point it was completely possible. "Did I do that in front of the kids?"

He looked down and nodded.

I left for a walk. I cried hard, realizing the amount of time I wasted imagining and believing that I really met Jesus.

The events of that night and day — the thoughts of Jesus Christ talking to me, The Plan, the birthday party — all of it was phony. Even the nurse I saw was not my friend Missy. This world of make believe was superimposed on the reality that those around me experienced. For example, my friend Catherine really did come to the door; only she was not a party guest, but a true friend who stopped over to keep my house together while Mike took me to a place to get well.

The only time I may have been with a higher power was when I prayed myself to sleep. The voices I attributed to Jesus with my distorted brain are inconsistent with a loving and caring God. Jesus didn't come to me that night; any higher power that may exist was with my family, friends and medical professionals who were working to expel these false notions from my brain. Mike recognized the insanity. He wasn't making plans for a party; he was scared and searching for someone or something that could help me.

A hallucination is what it was. It devoured me, and had it amassed from darker distortions could have killed me. I never experimented with hallucinogenic drugs. Because this was my first hallucination, it took a lot of time to convince me it didn't really happen. This distortion was only real in my own mind.

The medical staff who treated me called this loss of self a psychotic break. Regardless of how grand and joyous the events at times seemed, the realistic feeling visit with Jesus in a brand-new world built for me was an explosive series of hallucinations in a psychotic break. This traumatic, tragic, and, at times, blissful chaos had stretched across 36-48 hours, leaked into the following five days, and tempted me to return for months.

The peek-a-boo tricks of mental illness kept taunting me, tempting me back to the fantasy land. At the same time, the medications, medical psychologists and psychiatrists, and my family kept tugging me further into a place of sound mind. For every grain of sanity I collected, insanity would come back knocking at the door, inviting to take me under again.

Nonsense may be a word that trivializes the experience too severely, but it is the best English word to describe the string of activities that occurred when psychosis overtook me. I didn't know it at the time. I was high. I was traveling the world with Jesus by my side. I thought I was capable of grand change and influence in this world. I did think I was indestructible and unstoppable — fortunately, those around me didn't agree. They saw me out of control and loony. I was cartoony. I was speaking in rhymes. I was a grossly inflated distortion of myself; I was like a giant balloon soaring through the city streets at the Macy's Day parade. I was a grossly inflated distortion of myself. Like the hundreds of people pulling strings to parade a puffed-up popular character for onlookers on the street, I had my own team of puppeteers who tethered me home. I don't think they would put it that way, however; I think they thought they were merely helping me at a time when they feared there was no help at all.

It was a secret. There wasn't a big crowd watching me sail and soar. It wasn't for entertainment value. Each dose of medication was like puncturing my inflated self with a pin, slowly letting the air out. The real work was the pull of my family who kept visiting me in memory and in person. They reminded me of a place that was familiar, a place where I wasn't alone. They reminded me to come back.

I remembered something J.K. Rowling was quoted as saying at the Harvard Commencement Address in 2008: "Climbing out of poverty by your own efforts that is something on which to pride yourself, but poverty itself is romanticized only by fools." Similarly, I had been romanticizing insanity, trying to make it something beautiful and meaningful for nearly a year. The perspective of looking at it from the vantage point of another, rather than my own, had convinced me of the actual horror.

I remembered reading in Kay Redfield Jamison's book *An Unquiet Mind: A Memoir of Moods and Madness*, which explained her bipolar disorder in the context of her successful career as a psychiatrist, something like, to overcome the beast, one must first make it beautiful. I was convinced I was special and chosen to live with this disorder, and that it was a beautiful thing. I'd been a fool trying to assign meaning to it. Long ago, Dr. Burbach knew and told me to let it go. I wouldn't, or rather, couldn't heed the wise advice. I subscribed to the often-blurted phrase, "Everything happens for a reason." Searching for the reason of divinity handicapped my progress. The special lie I told myself was that bipolar made me more creative, more something good. A quick read of Wikipedia revealed many greats who lived with bipolar .... Patty Duke, Virginia Woolf, Vincent Van Gogh, Frank Sinatra, Axl Rose, Sinead O'Conner, Jack London, Earnest Hemmingway, Kurt Cobain. I wholeheartedly agreed with the information in the context of Jamison's earlier book *Touched with Fire: Manic-*

Depressive Illness and the Artistic Temperment, where she argued for a connection between bipolar disorder and artistic creativity.

Then I thought about the statistics that 2.6 percent of the U.S. population has been diagnosed with bipolar disorder, representing an estimated 5.5 million people. I was among the faceless. I was not special. I thought of Emily Dickinson's poem, "I'm nobody! Who are you?"

I had no idea how long I aimlessly walked our neighborhood streets. When I got home, I didn't look at anyone, I didn't say anything. I headed up the stairs to bed, covered myself with our thick burgundy comforter and tried to get the thoughts to end with a welcome, healing sleep.

Mike came to check on me.

"Are you okay?" he asked.

"I think I'm going to be," I said, as tears streamed silently down my cheeks. I swallowed the phlegm in my throat and muttered, "Thanks for taking care of me. I love you."

He leaned over my curled up body somewhat awkwardly from his seated position and wrapped his strong arms around me, pulling me into a secure embrace. I allowed him to protect me. I trusted his strength, knowing I had lost my own.

Winter Solstice

It was three days before Christmas Eve. The presents, hidden away from young eyes, waited to be wrapped. Snow was falling atop the ten inches already piled on the ground. The snow blower broke on just the third snowfall of the season; a replacement was bought on credit. The old one sat unused, broken, and clunky in our overfull one-car garage. School was not called off, however, so the older boys were in school. Alex played on the living room floor.

I was snuggled on the corner of the couch with my writing sweater hugging me, with a cup of lukewarm coffee at my side. I liked it that way: too hot and you lose the taste, too cold and you get a bitter chilly wash of filth in the mouth. Lukewarm, it was warm enough to offer the mouth the opportunity to taste it before it slid down the throat. The coffee was in a perfect mug; not too big and clunky or too small and dainty. The mug, about a half-inch thick, made it warm to the touch, comfortable. It was curved so the ceramic bevels outside the palm of the hand. This mug bore the commercial slogan stamped on its face, but it didn't mock me anymore. The slogan said, "Do what you like, like what you do: Life is Good!" A worthy — even in its mass production — message to start each day. And those days, I was doing what I liked: I was enjoying my family, writing in a journal, and working at the computer.

My youngest was mopping the floors. His toys were all overturned from their bins. The TV was off. We had two hours to wait until Thomas came home from school. That year, my middle son rode a bus to the public 4K program. We didn't have the money for tuition at the Montessori school, and we were too proud to accept a handout.

I knew if I went into the kitchen, I'd see the pictures Alex had colored earlier. Dishes needed attention, and I knew without looking that the laundry was piled up too. Yet, I sat and took in all the peace of the moment for a little longer.

Then, I made myself a bagel with cream cheese and strawberry jelly. My stomach settled without the help of Lorazepam. Since I only was working two days a week, my main responsibilities to give my life purpose involved watching the kids. I completed my undergraduate coursework a few months earlier. My degree was earned cum laude. I decided not to participate in the pomp and circumstance. Rather, I would just wait for the credential in the mail.

I got bored sometimes. While I was not really sick or sad or agitated, I did lack energy and was foggy some of the time. My limbs were heavy; naps were tempting. I wondered then if my medications were too high; I made a note to discuss this possibility with Dr. Carducci at my next appointment. I thought my body had healed enough from psychosis to function without so much chemical invasion.

Alex crawled on the floor with his blanket and looked up at the Christmas tree. Then deliberately, but silently, he made his way on hands and knees under the tree to plug in the lights. He then made his way back to his blanket, laid on the floor, snuggled the orange fleece, and admired the tree all aglow. Without light, the Christmas tree was just a blob of branches with things hung on them. The colored lights gave a tiny multi-colored glow amidst the branches highlighting the ornaments. The star shined most brightly. The ornaments revealed memories, recent and further in the past, a testament to generations and ritual. The apples were from Grandma Ann. The pipe cleaner candy canes were made from little hands. New this year, from Carol, were giant balls to freeze in time my and Thomas's roles in the local production of "The Christmas Carol." (I had never been in a play before, but when the director of the local production agreed to cast Thomas, she stated she would like to cast me as well. It was good to try something new, I thought. I had fun in the play, but also felt stretched beyond comfort enough to know I would never get onstage again.) All those trinkets hung dead until the light opened them to the eye. The lights woke the tree and gave life to the memories. Somehow at just age three, Alex realized this. Each morning he crawled to the outlet and plugged the strands in. He then sat back, and with a self-satisfied grin admired his work.

This Christmas, I was not tempted to attend church. Praying silently and selfishly, I pled to get myself through Christmas without feeling anxious, depressed, disappointed, frustrated, or anything else negative. I thought a lot about my family and all they sacrificed that year while I sat detached, trapped in my head. The clock's mechanical tick reminded me that time didn't stop for me. I realized I would never really know what happened during the past months in my children's lives. After being struck by mental illness, I could concentrate only on healing from it. This thing called time clicked by to mark the fleeting nature of a day, and at that winter solstice, an end of a season and nearly a year.

My job in Ozaukee County was scheduled to end at the conclusion of the calendar year. I had started a writing services business with Peggy, the woman who drove me home from the preschool that spring day I took my son to school on the bus. Since that day, I allowed her to take Thomas to her home for play dates with her only child. She obviously hadn't left her son in my care, and I didn't offer. I understood that I would probably not leave my own children in the care of someone else recovering from insanity either.

We once had a play date at a park with the boys when I mentioned my job ended in December and that I wasn't sure what I would do next.

Joining forces to start a business was her idea and it came via a text message.

"Do you want to start a business?" was typed on my phone screen.

"I don't know … maybe," I wrote back.

"What kind of business?" I sent another message, not waiting for a reply from the first.

"Not sure," she texted.

Strange, I thought then. I learned this woman was a counselor who worked at a transitional housing facility for recovering addicts. Peggy knew the whole story of my mental illness, at least as well as I could define it. Yet she wasn't afraid of me, wasn't afraid to start a business with me. I was still afraid of myself — to be trusted by another was humbling and healing. When we talked, she confided that she wanted to start a business and thought I might as well.

"What do you have in mind? Where did this come from?" I asked her.

"Well, I remember you saying that your job was ending in December," she said.

I thought about my retail store.

"Yeah, I do want to start a business. I actually have an idea," I told her.

I briefly summarized the Paper & Pen store idea to her, and she didn't tell me it was crazy. She seemed to thoughtfully mull it over. Her idea was to start a life coaching business, which I had no knowledge or interest in doing. We arranged to meet over a play date with the boys the following week.

In the course of several weeks, we decided on a business to open, partly by ruling out what we could not feasibly do.

The spreadsheets did not add up to open a retail store. My skills did not line up to do the coaching. So we decided to open a writing service business, offering grant writing, business writing, and editing. We formed an LLC, rented office space, and hung up an "open for business" sign. Fortunately, we already had a few leads on clients.

Also, Carol had agreed to stay on watching the boys twice a week while I worked at the business. She provided this child care generously and would not accept sufficient payment, which was good, because we did not have sufficient income to pay her. I was grateful and felt guilty all at the same time. I was learning not to be so hard on myself, and decided to just appreciate the good opportunities I had and to, as the saying goes, make the best of it. On that shortest day of the year, I decided to close the door on psychosis and just live normally. Not apologetically. Not timidly. Not foolishly. Just be normal.

Alcoholics

In the height of my anxiety, while under real and imagined stress, I got so angry at Mike. He was always calm, steady, and reasonable.

"Why are you so calm?" I asked him.

His answer was always the same: "Because I've had real problems, Tara."

That would infuriate me; the things I stressed about were "real" problems too, such as worrying about money, the kids' development, work, and my personal relationships. The mental breakdown landed in a whole other category. Its measure on the Richter magnitude scale was high and caused real damage, not just the fear and alarm caused by a small quake.

Mike is twenty years my senior. He had a whole life before we met when he was 47. I had no way of knowing or understanding the hardships he experienced. And these pages are not the space to explore them.

I had seen an old, dusty AA book on our bookshelf. Its glossy jacket cover long gone, the dull, hard-covered blue book sat on the shelf. Now and then, I picked it up and thumbed through its thick, hard pages, reading the table of contents and skimming through the headlined sections of the familiar 12-step program. I never read the book. I wondered about the man who bought it and kept it. Mike was not an alcoholic. He drank occasionally; alcoholics couldn't drink at all, I thought.

Shortly after we became familiar enough with one another for him to make himself at home while visiting, he had gone to my basement to get some beer to stock the refrigerator. Mike returned with a handful of bottles, a mix of Budweiser for him and Miller Lite for me.

"I know you are not an alcoholic," he said to me.

I knew he had seen the five cases of beer stacked in my basement, and I thought I heard sarcasm in his comment. What I thought he really meant was that I was an alcoholic because of my stockpile of beer. I started to explain about the party I had a few weeks before I met him and that I overbought at the time.

"How long ago was that?" he asked.

"About six weeks ago," I answered.

"If you were an alcoholic, this beer would be gone by now."

Another time, I asked Mike how much he drank when he was an alcoholic. I didn't understand how he could drink socially after going through AA. I thought there was an absolute sobriety requirement for alcoholics who had been through the program.

"All of it," he had answered me.

"All of it?"

"Yeah, whatever was there, I'd drink until it was all gone," he said.

Mike had compared my inpatient treatment and recovery to something of the experience of an addict recovery. In the hospital, I was given that little yellow pamphlet with the sobriety creed written on the back cover. Every time I saw it or thought about it, I had thought that lumping together those with mental illness with addicts was wrong. I believed that alcoholics inflicted their own pain, whereas mental patients were victims of circumstance.

Over the holidays, I ran into a cousin, yes I have a lot of cousins, I hadn't seen for years at a family party. I had heard she had had some problems with drug abuse, but I didn't know how severe it was. That's the thing about family. The life stories of its members are watered down as they are passed from aunt to sister to niece to cousin. She knew only that I had a "nervous breakdown" in the spring and I knew only that she was "in rehab" over the winter.

"How are you doing? I heard what happened to you," she told me. Each of us stood with a red solo cup filled with a white Russian mixed from Grandma Elaine's homemade Kahlua recipe — my family liked to drink.

I told her briefly of my experience and quickly turned the attention back to her.

"Should you be drinking?" I asked.

"Oh, alcohol was never my drug of choice," she said.

"Should you be drinking?" She asked back.

"Probably not," I admitted.

She told me about hitting rock bottom in Florida. It was the full-blown disaster: job loss, crippling debt, homelessness. She went to an ER unable to get a fix. Without insurance, they were able to place her in treatment, though this took several visits and being turned away many times until the severity of her situation couldn't be denied, and someone had to let her in and take care of her.

"So you were really crazy?" she asked again.

"Yeah," I said. "I guess I was."

"I felt so bad for those people in there," she said. "They would just sit and rock and have unfocused eyes. They were really gone."

I nodded, noting the irony that she thought those people had it worse than the addicts. I had thought the opposite. So they really lumped together these populations in an institutional setting. This conversation confirmed what I had assumed. Treatment for mental illness and drug/alcohol rehab occur within the same walls, halls of locked institutions.

I told her my diagnosis and that it was under good control. She assured me she will never return to life as an addict. We made promises to each ˙other, and really, to ourselves. I understood we hoped more than promised that we could keep those vows, since I accepted a prognosis for reoccurrence. We shared a supportive hug, and I carried the hope that we each could remain stable and healthy.

Afraid to Die

To me, the most troubling aspect of the bipolar diagnosis was that it was treatable, but not curable. The psychotic break was the event which prompted proper treatment for an ailment I carried throughout adult life.

It took a while to accept this diagnosis. Dr. Carducci had told me bipolar often has a genetic link. She had asked me questions regarding my immediate family; however, I could not confirm her suspicions. I could not recollect anyone who had been treated for mental illness in my immediate family. I knew for certain no one had been hospitalized. Like every family, there were a few members of the extended family who were a bit eccentric, but not so far to be considered insane.

I began to explore my family history, looking for the culprit who had passed down the gene that caused it. First, I examined my parents. Mom and Dad had been married for 38 years; they were high school sweethearts who married at age 17 and never left each other's side. One time, my dad told me he would be happy anywhere with any amount of accommodations as long as my mother was with him.

So I looked sideways. My sister was as predictable as a sunrise. Billie wanted to be a teacher since she was a young child and played school with me during our free time together. She was a good student, labeled a pleasure to have in class, and made the dance squad in high school. She hung out with the popular crowd, worked part time, always had money to spend, and managed to purchase her own car at age 16. As far as I could see, she remained steady with no symptoms of mental illness from her youth on into adulthood. She went on to college at the traditional age and graduated with a degree in special education, later earning a master's degree in the subject, and worked in the field for nearly two decades.

I had one cousin, who was really a second cousin once removed, who had bipolar disorder and was diagnosed as a teenager, but I didn't see this cousin much, and the connection seemed to be too distant to include in a genetic picture. Maybe the genetic link was wrong. I soon exhausted of this traveling through my lineage, decided it was unproductive, and went instead to examine my own life.

I found a child who always struggled in school and a teenager who always hung with trouble. There was a clear instability in my work life; I bounced from job to job, rarely finding satisfaction. And, there was the rage and distorted perceptions. This rage was the most difficult to accept, but also the biggest part of my personality that I would like to change. Maybe it wasn't just a mannerism, maybe this fight against real and imagined injustice in me was really a manifestation of an unstable mood disorder.

I was scared of bipolar because I was scared I might become psychotic on a regular basis. I was scared my children would develop it. I was scared I might lose my children. I was scared I might become so far removed from society that I would be tucked away in an institution with just infrequent visits from people of my past who would find it in themselves to care about me.

I thought I almost died during the psychotic break. I wasn't really dying, but I held the belief that I was for some time. The only thing that kept me going was the idea that God needed me here on earth for some reason. I dabbled with the idea that maybe I was supposed to write this book, to help people understand what mental illness was like.

I was a writer. I wrote to hold a fleeting piece of truth; I wrote with honesty. I wrote in exchange for an income. On good days, of which there were more lately, I believed writing was my vocation. Mike supported this, both as the breadwinner and as the gentle encourager. When I worked on the craft, I found peace. I believed writing was a reasonable pursuit. I lacked confidence, and holding a diagnosis that has crippled so many didn't help. This missing confidence cannot be manufactured; it could only develop through practice.

I was afraid I would join the ranks of people who died at their own hands as a result of bipolar disorder. I recognized I have a piece of the good life, although I couldn't always feel it. Intellectually, I knew I was fortunate. Emotionally, I often still felt doomed. In the wake, I also felt tarnished with a diagnosis of the weak.

If I died at my own hands, I would miss Mike — the only man I ever needed. He held me up and challenged me to live a better life. I would miss spring time: the greening of the grass, the lengthening of days, the sound of activity returning after a dormant winter of chilled silence. I would miss food: chocolate, steak, ice cream, shrimp, blueberry smoothies, baked potatoes.

While I didn't die or contemplate suicide after the psychosis, I knew I left earth and was traumatically ill. I didn't ask for my kids; I only wanted Mike. I really only needed Mike. I didn't know how that happened. I was not sure when he became my entire world, but I knew I was lost without him. If I died, the only feeling I would miss would be his embrace. I would regret more than I would miss, and I realized I needed to start living more of a life that I would miss.

Circumstance & Faith

So who was to blame for this disease, this disease that came with a risk of suicide?

Dr. Burbach explained the theory of genetic link for bipolar disorder to me.

"There is an underlying propensity, which was always there," he said. "The trigger was the expression of the disease."

Epigenetic was another word he used. It meant the approximately stepwise process by which genetic information, as modified by environmental influences, was translated into the substance and behavior of an organism. The environmental influences he identified as stress, and not the stress you would think. It wasn't the death of a spouse or loved one. It wasn't the type that makes the top stressors on any list. Rather, the stress he referred to was the accumulation of relatively typical kind of day-to-day stressors.

Dr. Burbach explained the age of the diagnosis was not the true age of onset. There was an underlying propensity that was always there. I had the bipolar gene, so to speak. The index episode, which prompted the diagnosis, was the hospitalization-requiring incident of psychosis. However, in a less severe form the disease manifested before then. The rage was the obvious symptom, the depression another. The mild mania was another.

This all sounded very rational; it made logical sense to believe these researched stories and move forward from these scientific conclusions. I had to remain faithful to the medicine. I was frightened enough of going through it again to believe bipolar and stick with the program. It was impossible to deny the diagnosis. I always knew there was something that caused my brain to betray me and construct elaborate scenes of distortion.

The reaction of my family when I suffered from psychosis also scared me. I recognized my episode of psychosis as a sickness. While I sought medical treatment, I relied on my faith in a higher power. I prayed constantly to never again experience psychosis. I did rosaries for myself before bed, counting the beads on my fingers. I started collecting rosaries. I also collected angels, because my grandmother Ann told me she believed in them and couldn't put away her Christmas angels. That was my last conversation with her.

"I need to believe in the angels," she had said during her hospice care.

Now that I was diagnosed with my own chronic illness, I needed more than the science and logic. I talked to God. I prayed for others. I constantly attempted to reach God. I begged Him for health. I begged him to let me live.

Eventually, I convinced myself that God helps those who help themselves, and by accessing proven health care solutions, I was doing just that. I considered these physicians, and their pharmaceuticals, as people created by God to help people, like me, who live chronically with mental illness.

My doctors told me some people live "normal" lives with ups and downs and are able to manage these variances without rage and despair. Healthy people did not cry at the slightest emotional trigger. They did not scream at the mildest of infractions. These "normal" people reacted to life's curveballs rationally — they still got nervous, excited, happy, sad, angry, frustrated, or any other range of emotion. On the medicine, I also experienced a range of feelings. I just no longer experienced irrational emotions or reacted with out-of-place behavior. If I was sad, I could still take a shower and get the kids breakfast; without medicine, when I was sad, I couldn't get out of bed or get the thoughts that the world would be better off without me to stop.

My doctors convinced me I had a disease. One of my main concerns was that they may be wrong. Was it possible to entrust a higher power solely to save me and help me live the life I was meant to live without the poisons of medication? The answer was I couldn't possibly know, but I found the resources of information from scientists to be the most logical avenue toward health. I found the comforts of theology to be the most logical path to grace, but without health there could be no peace.

I found reassurance in the old story of the man on the roof. A man was stranded on his roof following the devastation of a flood, so he prayed for God to save him. A boat came by, but he dismissed the assistance, faithful that God would save him. Another boat came, and the man's reaction was the same. A helicopter flew over, and the man again was steadfast in his faith that God would save him. Just before he died, he asked God why He didn't save him, and God told the man that He sent him two boats and a helicopter, and there was nothing else He could do to save him. God — if there is one — provided people who are passionate about researching and treating mental illness, and accepting this explanation was the only thing I could do to save myself and reconcile both faith and logic.

Scientists provided mankind with the tools to higher living. Theology was another gift, but not powerful enough on its own to explain the workings of the natural world. I trusted the organic knowledge of the doctors. I realized they may have been wrong. It was based on faith that I would not become a statistic of suicide, would not become a tragedy.

When I decided to genuinely call my illness bipolar and accept the lifelong treatment set forth by my doctors, I achieved balance and sustainable productivity in my life. I made an income with my a writing services business. I also was the primary caregiver for the family.

My husband counted on me to stick with the program. Mike deserved a healthy life partner; after all, my recovery was more of him giving than receiving and that was not a sustainable recipe for a lasting marriage. He deserved to be with a spouse who could contribute. I clutched this belief so tightly it kept me on my medications. I tried not to toy with the idea that I could manage on my own, without the medication. I tried not to give in to the feelings that I could develop enough willpower to protect myself and my family from the dangers of mental illness, namely bipolar. I remembered my children; then, I remembered the stories I have read of those who grew up in homes with mentally ill parents who went untreated. My children deserved a healthy and coherent mother. They deserved to grow up in a safe and consistent home where they could flourish unaffected by mental illness. My children needed me strong. They were fragile and couldn't be expected to carry the burden of having an unstable parent. My children and their needs kept me on the program, too.

I recognized Christians all around me. Their lives seemed secure and safe. They had a shelter to the evils of the world. Mental illness was the evil that resided inside me. I thought of the Savior, the Creator, and Holy Spirit as a "higher power." I didn't dismiss the views of those from other religions; I believed everyone had the chance to live with the spirit of a higher power guiding their path. Jews, Muslims, Christians, Hindus, and others all could be correct in their determination of divinity. This power of a creator to me became indefinable, and that became okay with me. I was at peace knowing that I could never know. Like there are many roads that lead to California, there are plenty of paths leading to grace. I gave up the hunt for certainty and decided instead to appreciate life and love.

At this point, I saw no other choice: I became agnostic. I knew I didn't meet Jesus during the episode of psychosis. I did not know for sure if He existed, but it really stopped mattering to me. I saw my transformation from an angst-filled, desperate person to a woman who grew into grace. I found stability after being stripped to a raw nothingness.

My doctors reassured me, saying that with continued, life-long treatment and medication, I would do well. I took a handful of medications each day. I took Lamictal: 400 mg — taken in two 200 mg doses — one in the morning and one at bedtime. I took Abilify, an antipsychotic, taken as 10 mg pill at bedtime. My doctors and I once tried to wean me off this pill. We went down to 7.5 mg and then tried to go down to 5. In a rage, I smashed that ridiculously large-screen TV.

My favorite pill remained Lorazepam. It was my little helper; just a couple milligrams taken as needed (no more than four a day) to keep the anxiety away. I took it in the morning to ease my children's before school routine. I took it at lunch or in the afternoon to keep my mind from reeling. I took it when I socialized, because I panicked that people judged me. I touched my tongue to the roof of my mouth to spread the pill's chalky, melting morsels. I filled my cheeks with saliva, gently swallowed, and waited for that calming feeling that let me not panic.

On the medications, my world was okay. I found my grace. Apart from them, I failed to live beautifully. I swallowed the pills regularly and prayed I wasn't crazy.

Global Assessment of Findings

As the one-year anniversary of my hospitalization approached in March, I was ready to face the entire truth of it. I hadn't seen Dr. Burbach for about four months, but I made an appointment. I wanted a final assessment of what happened and where I could go from there. I remembered crying on the corner of his couch as I wondered if I'd find a way to belong. I remembered his patience and kindness as he talked me through my perceived and real problems while offering encouragement and hope.

As it turned out, I didn't have a textbook case of bipolar disorder, but the presumption was I had some form of it. My symptoms did not fit neatly in the classification parameters. I had a Mood Disorder, Not Otherwise Specified (NOS), mixed with a history of psychotic features. This diagnosis had five axes. The first was the NOS. The second were my personality traits and the third were my physical medical problems — hypothyroidism in my case. The fourth were stressors, which were something I could somewhat control. The final axis was the global assessment of findings, which was my capacity to function in the world.

However, the diagnosis did not imply severity. Bipolar was a spectrum disorder with many variants from mild to borderline and severe to incapacitating. The distress and impairment I experienced during psychosis and the immediate weeks and months following were incapacitating, but the manifestations earlier in the disease's lifespan were mild to moderate. It climaxed without me knowing it was

246

there, catching me off guard. From that point forward, it demanded attention, classification, treatment, and respect. I simply could not go on any longer as a person who just needed to try harder. The internal medical problem, although mental in nature, would need medical attention — chronically so.

The hospitalization did not result from an isolated incident. It could be placed in the context of a lifetime of mood instability. During childhood and adolescence, it was presented in outbursts, slamming, breaking things, and aggressive and destructive elements. There was rapid cycling, which was an instability of extremes. The next day's phenomenon featured denial, avoidance, and minimizing.

I couldn't help but worry about my symptoms and fear their return, although they hadn't returned except that incident when I broke a TV after lowering my medication. Because I had one experience, there was a higher likelihood that I will become again psychotic, but bipolar was not a death sentence, and my doctors predicted the likelihood of my becoming psychotic again as minimal. There were some ways to increase my chance at normal life, symptom free.

At the end of the visit, Dr. Burbach made a list of things that helped my prognosis:
•Treatment compliance.
•Adaptive resources.
•Supportive family.
•Job skills.
•Absence of drugs and alcohol abuse.
•Absence of legal problems.
•Spirituality.

Treatment compliance meant I followed all the prescribed recommendations for recovery. I took my medications; I went to all my scheduled appointments. I read the recommended reading. I never swayed from the program, though plenty of times I got angry at the disease and wanted to pull myself off the medications and find an alternative way to live with the disease. But I did not. I didn't let doubt of the disorder trump my faith in the professionals who knew how to save me from having it devour me and set loose the footholds in my life. The treatment changed as I did; I saw Dr. Carducci quarterly to monitor my medications. In addition to the frightening rage when I smashed the television set, I had breakthrough mild symptoms. Depression came mildly that winter, causing excessive sleepiness, a lack of motivation, and feelings of worthlessness. I had learned when the simple daily task of showering was too much to bear, I may be struggling with depression, so I took care of it: I contacted Dr. Carducci, and she adjusted my medication.

When Dr. Burbach said adaptive resources, I figured he meant I had creativity. I found a way to not only live with bipolar, but live well within its context.

Supportive family couldn't be denied. Especially Mike. My parents, who I never fully appreciated until the hindsight exploration of my childhood, supported me. It couldn't have been easy raising me, but they never wavered in their support of me or love for me. Also there was Carol, who tangibly stepped into the role of caregiver for my children when I returned to work or went to my doctor appointments, and she read my writing. My children gave me purpose and unconditional love. I was surrounded not only by family, but also supportive friends.

Job skills were tangible. Despite my lack of stability in a work setting, I garnered enough knowledge and skills to contribute to a company. I also managed to complete my undergraduate degree during recovery. It wouldn't have been possible without the treatment compliance.

Being clean from drugs and alcohol was a plus, but it was difficult to forgo alcohol completely in social settings.

Sometimes, I drank an old fashion or a glass of wine. Sometimes, I binged and drank too much. Regarding drugs, I never really used them.

No legal problems: I guess some people with bipolar had it worse. I fortunately never reached this extreme. I remembered reading a story about a woman who bit off her husband's tongue in a manic state. She now has a criminal record. The world laughed at this story as its absurdity appeared in the local paper. I didn't. I felt empathy. I knew. I understood — it could have been me. Without treatment of the disease, she lost herself, her logic, and her control over her own actions. Yet, rightfully so, she was held accountable for her actions.

Regarding the spirituality, I believed in something beyond me and those supporting me. I believe God resided outside of us, but also within us. We all have the capacity to feel peace and share compassion, and that, in my mind, is a gift.

With the benefit of a proper diagnosis and treatment, the range of emotions was more diverse and more level. I became neither zombielike nor neurotic. I blended in as normal — bipolar could have remained a secret that no one would have suspected. Indeed, when I told people I had bipolar who didn't know me before, they didn't believe me. Stability improved my life dramatically. I walked lighter, free from the weight of the worry. Circumstance was something I could create, and I learned to take control by letting go.

I was not always free from the symptoms of bipolar disorder. Believing mental illness required releasing the hallucinations, the memories of which visited me and attempted to shake me from steady ground. I fought the symptoms — but not alone: I trusted science and medicine, and included doses of conversation and loving support, to reach a sliver of peace. I couldn't keep peace; I couldn't clutch it tight. Like everyone, I recognized its presence and smiled at it and willed it to stay.

I stopped feeling sorry for myself for having to live with this disorder. I came to believe that each of us was living under suboptimal conditions. Christians believed we all had a cross to bear; their comfort was in knowing that Jesus only gives us as much as we can carry. Scientists agreed for every force in nature there was an equal and opposite force. The disease bipolar was my cross or my negative force. My strength was adequate to bear this, and my vision was to do so with beauty.

Dr. Burbach told me to think of it as physical medical problem affecting the brain. The example he used was a diabetic who took insulin and modified his diet. But I didn't think his explanation really rang true, because insulin-dependent diabetes didn't come with the stigma. Society accepted it as out of one's control. I felt guilty for having this bipolar, but I was only responsible for my actions — not of the disease itself. I wanted to try to be mentally tough, but my brain was fragile and needed stabilizing medications. I felt I did something wrong to deserve it, but my transgressions are no worse than those people without mental illness. I was told there was a biological and genetic link to explain it, although this didn't begin to address the why. The cliché of mind over matter didn't work for me, because my brain was the matter that organically was flawed. I had to use my intelligence to accept this theory and function as a person with a form of bipolar disorder.

My ability to pretend to belong was a self-preserving mechanism and explained why I was able to make it to age 33 before the disease manifested in a way so severe it could no longer be ignored. People who loved me saw me as separate from my disease. My husband told me that it wasn't me when the depression inhabited my soul or the mania sent me in crazy directions. My sister said there always had been a visitor from something beyond me that manifested itself in unclear thinking and distorted ideology. My mother simply said the diagnosis made sense and explained a lot.

I feared I was bipolar and that was all there is of me. I feared I was unable to find a place of rest and purpose in this world, because I have so often lost touch of reality. The delusions I held were so convincing, I sometimes struggled to know what to accept and what to dismiss. That was perhaps the scariest part: my perceptions couldn't always be trusted and I couldn't always tell the difference between what was real and imagined.

Accepting bipolar as a valid chronic condition and navigating the world with grace as a person who was clinically mentally ill will take a lifetime. Most of the time, I was okay. And really that was all anyone could have or request.

I had a mental illness. It was not just a case of the blues or an episode of extravagance. It was something rooted with a firm grasp attempting to rob my sanity. Many doctors think the word bipolar offered a better description of the teeter-totter of symptoms than the previous label of manic depressive. It was classified in the mood-disorder family. With bipolar disorder, the pendulum swung from a hopeless pole to mania, each side a welcome respite from the other. Back and forth seemed more accurate than up and down, but it was a mixed bag of extremes that often swirled together.

Without a measuring stick, doctors probed, jabbed, and questioned. As they found commonalities to their lists, they made educated assumptions. Believing their assessment gave me the path to hope and health; the alternative hurt too much. Denial, a cousin to the disorder, tempted logic. Denial's attraction was to believe instead this category of sickness was hogwash. It classified the previous description as weakness. It served to forgo a scientific treatment and rather prescribed to dress with gumption and arm with willpower a way without treatment. I kept hope. I trusted those who loved me, when I knew not to trust myself. Momentarily, however, I was okay.

Yet, the disease crippled my attempts. It came uninvited to destroy my footholds. It was the tide that washed away a sandcastle, the wind that eroded the stone, the sun that faded the colors, or the locusts that devoured the crops. This disease visited and stayed and destroyed. Then poof — it vanished, leaving me guilty of its destruction. It was not poetic. It was unapologetic. It robbed me of dignity. It disgraced me with humiliation. It made my travels burdensome.

Pain was a funny thing. Oftentimes, it was the makings of our own minds that caused the hurting. For the better part of a year, I held the idea that there were two options: accepting bipolar as a life-long problem, or discovering the incident and diagnosis were some kind of mistake. It turned out the resolution was a bit less concrete, and the acceptance of the disease was filled with shades of gray. Like a bone stress fracture that heals over time, so did my mind. It was nearly as if the break never happened. Recovery was difficult and long and full of setbacks. The only evidence that remained of the fracture was memory. Memories stamped in the pages of this narrative, and on medical charts in dusty storage file drawers. There was also the daily reminder of the pillbox, which held the contents of health.

The psychosis and the path from there to wellness were just a place I once visited. It was a place I left behind as I returned to the person I always was, only different. I was stronger, less vulnerable, and more confident. Taken out of the context of a life sentence, I placed the breakdown in a chapter of life that has ended. It is not a cross that I bear that weighs me down. The breakdown was a turning point that set me free.

Sanity was a fleeting place of grace. Peace can stay if only one can learn to stay in the day: Not looking ahead or behind, just stillness in the moment. I wrote this poem in a journal:

Acceptance
I thought I was
Chasing Sanity
When all I needed
Was clarity
I have healed (for now)
And realized
Love is all around me
But this emotion, I could not feel
Or hold onto
My chance to clasp peace
Fleeting before me

Liking Me

Thomas, in all seriousness, said to me, "I like you better now."

I swallowed and gave him a smile. Then I nodded, pulling him into a hug while squeezing back an escaping heavy tear. With the embrace I held too long, I silently promised to keep this person that I had become intact.

"Me too, Thomas. Me too," I said.

He looked up at me and seemed to believe I would remain strong and healthy and there for him. He was secured in my love. He went to play as I excused myself to the bathroom.

In the mirror I saw a swollen, blotchy face. In this privacy, I allowed the grieving tears to freely flow. I mourned the life I did not live as I should. I cursed the transgressions that I caused while untreated. With a soft wash cloth, I dampened my face. I was amazed at how physically unchanged I looked. To the world, to those who didn't know, I was unchanged. To those who really knew, I was transformed.

I liked myself better. I was secure in a place of mental healthiness. I had regained some resemblance of stability. I had hope. My days were pretty boring, yet I appreciated each one with renewed respect.

It wasn't all joy. I lived with a chronic, low-grade fear of myself and what I was capable of doing. I was humbled by the realization of the fragility of life, control, and relationships. These abstract constructs of life were what made living rich, worthwhile, and relevant. My fear was that I would again succumb and tear right down to the foundation, and have all that was good crumble and disappear once more. I feared that I would be left with only memories of all that was good.

This concern was a constant running in the background of my mind — a whisper that reminded and motivated me to work to keep delicate happiness. While I couldn't deny this possibility, I had to believe in the rarity of it actualizing with continued treatment. I had surrendered to a lifetime of treatment. And just when I thought again the disease was hogwash and that I could live without treatment, I was terrorized by flashbacks and nightmares.

These nightmares came in a recurring dream. In these dreams, I was trapped and chased and the only way to escape was to levitate and fly. I flew in beautiful swirls like a ballerina. Only eventually, inevitably I lost my control. I began to thrash and fly in crazy directions at dangerous speeds, like a plane about to crash. I awoke in the still, dark night. By reflex, I sat straight up. I panted. I was covered in sweat. I woke Mike by calling his name in a panic. He was steady, committed. Wrapping his strong arms around me, he drew me onto his chest.

He repeated, "It's okay. It's okay. You are okay."

He stroked my hair like I was child; when he heard my breath quicken, he pulled me back into a tight hold. He protected me against the dangers of my own mind. He offered calmness and steadiness and strength. I was grateful. I needed his protection.

Once, I had a dream that was even worse. I drove a car off a cliff. Impulsively, I cranked the wheel to steer the car into the woods below. In the next scene in the dream, I was walking near a makeshift camp, living happily, stupidly off the land. Then a neighbor hillbilly type found me and told me

Mike was coming to get me. The scene when Mike arrived was the scariest. He said I was manic again, that I was too dangerous to be around my children. I tried to run. He used his strong arms to again secure me, only this time to trap me rather than to protect me. He brought me to a mental hospital and told me that is where I had to live.

Dr. Carducci said these were just nightmares. She advised me to not store them to memory, to not believe them. Yet, despite this advice, the memory of my night tremors lurked. The horrors stuck inside my mind. And just when I thought I was over it — that I was finally and completely free of bipolar — another nightmare came.

This was where surrendering to a higher power must come in. I knew Mike may not always be there. I knew I was not strong enough to live without help. I knew the medication could only intervene with the faulty chemistry of my brain. I knew lifestyle choices and psychotherapy were only illusions of control. While I committed to a lifetime of science-based treatment and therapy, I resolved to trust in a higher power — God, if that makes you understand —— to protect and love me.

When Thomas told me he liked me better, I remembered where I had been and recognized where I could go. I prayed for the me I had become to stay.

Yes, Thomas, I was better. Please, I pled to the abyss, let me always be better. Let this healthy now last.

About the Author

Tara Meissner is a former journalist and a lifelong creative writer. She holds a Bachelor of Arts Degree and works part-time at her local library. Tara lives in Wisconsin with her husband, Mike, and their three sons. She writes longhand in composition notebooks. Stress Fracture: A Memoir of Psychosis is her first book. Visit her online at www.tarameissner.com